The New Breed

The New Breed

Actors Coming of Age

Photographed, Edited, and with an Introduction by Karen Hardy
Interviews and Text by Kevin J. Koffler
Design and Cover by Wesley Anderson

An Owl Book
HENRY HOLT AND COMPANY
NEW YORK

**I dedicate this book to
every person who *has the
courage* to be themselves
and pursue their dreams
for true reasons.
I support you.**

Published by Henry Holt and Company, Inc.,
115 West 18th Street, New York, New York 10011.

Published in Canada by Fitzhenry & Whiteside Limited,
195 Allstate Parkway, Markham, Ontario L3R 4T8.

Library of Congress Cataloging-in-Publication Data
Hardy, Karen.
   The new breed.
   "An Owl book."
   1. Motion picture actors and actresses—United States
—Biography.   2. Motion picture actors and actresses—
United States—Portraits.   I. Koffler, Kevin J.
II. Title.
PN1998.2.H37   1988   791.43'028'0922   [B]   88–1933
ISBN 0-8050-0774-1 (pbk.)

First Edition

Designer: Wesley Anderson

Printed in the United States of America

10 9 8 7 6 5 4 3 2 1

ISBN 0-8050-0774-1

CONTENTS

INTRODUCTION

THE NEW BREED represents a new consciousness whereby we pursue our dreams for the right reasons—for art, for truth, for self fulfillment, sharing and honest communication rather than the superficial, fame, fortune and glamour. Some of the actors in this book talk about apathy in the world, of our getting lost in our image. We live, especially in America, in such an image-conscious society. We work so hard to fit in, to belong. Even those of us who are non-conformist labor on our images.

Our identities have been manipulated by the bombarding images of the media. We have lost the essence of who we are. The actors interviewed here are fighting to retain their integrity in an industry notorious for it's manipulation of image, identity and self worth. In this book they have revealed who they truly are and what they really want and believe in.

A few years ago I started getting lost in the image I had created for myself. No one could break through my wall, at one point, not even myself. I got caught in the wave. I didn't really care about politics or what went on in the wider world, because I didn't honestly feel I could do anything to affect change. Living in New York City, I would sometimes see someone suffering, cold, alone on the street and I would feel their pain which compounded my feeling of helplessness and ineffectiveness. And yet, within my social life, I pursued what I thought was my own cool sense of style. I thought I was my own person, yet I was lost within myself. I had lost the child in me who had dreams, who wanted to love and needed love in return.

I remember going to see an afternoon show of *River's Edge*, a film about apathy in youth in America, at the Waverly Cinema in Greenwich Village. There was a scene in which a boy brings his friends into the woods to see the naked, dead body of a girlfriend with whom they had all grown up. He had killed her. They hardly reacted. There was no emotion, no remorse, nothing. In the horror of the moment, I realized that I, too, felt nothing. The theater was only a few blocks from my apartment building;

as I started home, uncontrollable tears flooded me. I cried all the way home. I couldn't stop. I realized then that I am a part of the world and of other human beings—that I do care. By caring, I *can* make a difference. It was an awakening for me. Tears of pain turned to tears of happiness. The moment reaffirmed for me my love of film and my appreciation of a medium that can touch and educate as well as entertain.

I had come to a point where I had to look at myself and decide whether I really could go through with **THE NEW BREED**, whether I was willing to commit to it, or let go and move on. I had searched my soul. When I decided it was something I wanted and *had* to do, I realized, that in order to get it, I'd have to crack open that wall I'd built up for security. The wall which had become a safe retreat from the world and my own feelings. The wall which was preventing me from communicating and taking action.

My approach to this book is to let people tell their real story. Our media depict picture-perfect images where reality is often distorted. The truth is that we all have our individual struggles, whether it be with our families, our peers, or our financial positions. It is important that we accept and support each other for who we really are, not for the distorted profiles we've been taught our whole lives to project. The process actors have to go through in searching their souls and establishing their true identities is one we can all learn from.

The actors in this book have bared their souls and shared their pain, their dreams and their hopes for the future. Their approach toward their craft may differ from individual to individual, but the common thread that holds them together is an unwavering commitment to following their instincts and a pursuit of excellence that enables each to transcend the prevailing mediocrity and myth of the Hollywood machine.

I give you a new consciousness and awareness—THE NEW BREED . . .

KAREN HARDY

Willem Dafoe

There is a powerful energy emanating from Willem Dafoe; the intensity he brings to the stage and screen is flowing from a place embedded deep in his character. Dafoe has evolved into the consummate actor's actor of the new breed. He is respected by his peers for the diverse roles he accepts and the sense of honesty he brings to them, as well as his passionate commitment to creating vernal landscapes and provoking unfaded ideas.

Dafoe transcends conventional categorization. His probity as an actor has allowed him to create a space all his own. Although he has achieved critical and popular acclaim as a movie star in feature films like *Platoon* and *To Live and Die in L.A.*, Dafoe remains very involved in the Wooster Group, an avant-garde experimental theater workshop located in Manhattan's Soho district and run by Elizabeth Le Compte, Dafoe's live-in lover and the mother of his son Jack.

A multi-media endeavor utilizing videos, audio recordings and live action, the Wooster Group merges its members' personal pasts with cultural and historical happenings. The results are often bizarre, intriguing and controversial. The company offers its audiences the possibility of experiencing theater in an entirely new way by providing the opportunity to examine life from a different perspective.

If Dafoe accomplishes any one thing in his work, it's to open up the viewer. He seeks to make a difference by encouraging his audience to interpret his work and apply what they learn and what they feel to their own lives. Dafoe's priority as an actor is to have fun, but he is just as committed to getting people to think.

WHAT WAS YOUR CHILDHOOD LIKE?

I pretty much block out my childhood. Let's see . . . The house I grew up in seemed very big to me. It was a classic white house, brick, with a two-car garage next door. Our property bordered on farm land. When I was a kid, you could walk 30 feet out of my house and you were in a farmer's field. My father was a surgeon, but the neighborhood was distinctly middle class. It was on the outskirts of Madison, Wisconsin, in an area that was just starting to get built up. As I grew up, it got built up very quickly.

WHEN DID YOU DECIDE TO BECOME AN ACTOR?

When I was very young. It was something I enjoyed doing as a kid. I was sort of a cut-up. I came from a family of eight kids, and when you come from a large family, you have to find your identity and your turf in that family. When I was a kid—and even now, to some degree—I had some facility for mimicry, so I was kind of crudely the joker, the practical joker. I was the kid who would get his attention by doing gags. That kind of naturally led to writing plays as a child.

DO YOU REMEMBER THE FIRST PLAY YOU EVER WROTE?

Yeah, I do. I called it "The Alaskan Gold Rush." I liked history when I was a kid; I still do. I used to write these plays that were historical dramas. They were very funny. About 15 years ago, I ran across some of them. The scenes were very lean, and the difficulty I had was extending scenes; I always wanted to get to the action. The scenes were like, "Hey Jeb, get me a cup of coffee. Hey Jeb, I hear there's been some claim jumpers around here," and then there would be a big fight that would last for three minutes. I was really into the action.

WHAT WAS YOUR FIRST ROLE?

That was it.

WHAT WAS YOUR FIRST PROFESSIONAL ROLE?

It depends what you consider professional. If you consider professional to be when I was making a living at it, as opposed to summer stock, it was with a group called Theater X. I was about 18 then. My first role was actually a lot of different roles in a series of vignettes. The company is based in Milwaukee, Wisconsin, but in the two or three years I was with them, we were very seldom there. We had the good fortune of hooking up with a very good producer in Europe, and we performed there a lot.

WHY DID YOU LEAVE THEATER X AND MOVE TO NEW YORK CITY?

Theater X developed and created their own work. The money I made was enough to live on, but it was really hard work. It was as much of a lifestyle as anything else. I've always been ambitious, and it was frustrating, so I went to New York City, fully intending to become a commercial actor.

WHAT HAPPENED WHEN YOU GOT THERE?

I looked around, and between what I was interested in, and what was available to me, nothing was really happening. I found myself going downtown to see performances. I had always been very curious about the Performance Group and Richard Forman's group, so I knocked around. I went to go see a performance called "Rumstick Road" by the Wooster Group. I couldn't make heads or tails out of it, but the performers were really good, the performance was exciting and the place felt very important. I gravitated towards that. I started hanging out and working as an actor in the Performance Group, started watching the development of a new show and eventually I became a regular member of the Wooster Group.

WHAT WAS THE DIFFERENCE BETWEEN THE WOOSTER GROUP AND THEATER X?

The work was very different, and also the people were a lot older in the Wooster Group. The thrust was also very different. In Theater X, we were essentially working with a playwright, where in the Wooster Group, we work much more in collage, with elements that already exist, and play with them.

DO YOU UNDERSTAND WHAT THE WOOSTER GROUP'S WORK MEANS NOW?

No I don't, which is fine. I do in glimpses, and sometimes, if I think really hard, I can get a really snappy line down, but it always defeats the whole purpose because I find myself often changing my mind about how we work.

WHAT SHOULD A PERSON GET FROM WATCHING A WOOSTER GROUP PERFORMANCE?

Sometimes people have trouble watching things and accounting for them. When the structure is very familiar to them, they can elicit the appropriate emotional response, and there's kind of a pleasure in that. We all know classic play structures. We all know plays with a very strong narrative; that's easy to relate to, because most people have been brought up on television, catharsis and all literary traditions. This stuff is much easier to watch if you view it as you would dance or a painting. It is what it is. That's not to say it's unstructured; it's very structured. That's not to say it's unintelligible; it's very intelligible. It just doesn't hit you or stack up in a classic psychological way. It's basically abstract. When you say abstract, people kind of check out because they think it's not going to mean anything to them or it's not going to be fun, but that's simply not true. The closest thing you can say you want from an audience is that you want them to enjoy being there, and have it be a special place. I'm not sure everyone would agree with me, but to me it's that feeling of creating a special landscape that doesn't exist. I like plays and realism just as much as the next guy, but to me this is a little more interesting, because it's not an imitation of something—it is what it is. It's like making something out of thin air from stuff around you and making something new.

DO YOU TRY TO DO THAT WITH ALL YOUR WORK?

Sort of. I like it when your personal history sort of runs parallel to your fictional history, and they sort of crisscross each other every once in a while; it all feels like the same thing, and it's very exciting. That's why, when I'm making a film, I respond to exotic locations and interesting people. It's just about doing stuff that interests you, making things you don't know about and doing things you've never done before—things you don't *know* you don't know—and that's exciting. It's an elevated experience in the fact that it is a movie or a performance, and it allows a frame and a structure to take all that experience to pour it all into. That's what any performance is: that kind of reflection, that kind of meditation on what is happening in my life next to this structure.

HOW DO YOU FEEL ABOUT THE MAJORITY OF SCRIPTS YOU ARE SUBMITTED?

I'm better at telling what is bad than what is good. Sometimes there is a real clarity there I like, but a lot of scripts are just fishing around and are totally effect-oriented. A lot of scripts are just too vague. They're not articulate; they're generic. With a script, it's about vision, it's about a special thing. It's about, do you want to invest yourself in this little activity that is this script? I read it and ask myself, do I want to do these things?

WHAT DO YOU LOOK FOR IN A SCRIPT?

I look for fun stuff to do, and to some degree, a character I feel an affinity for but may not necessarily be. It's mostly about doing fun stuff, though. I see what the character has to do, I see how the scenes play, and I say, do I want to do that? Would that be interesting to me? Would that create some sort of vibration in me that would be interesting?

HOW DO YOU PREPARE FOR A ROLE ONCE YOU'VE ACCEPTED IT?

That varies terrifically. It depends who you're working with and where you're shooting. I really ease into it. I hear stories

about how actors prepare, and everyone's different, but I can't get programmed. It's always nice to get an activity or a physical thing that's fun to do that brings you closer to your character. Professions are fun. When I did *To Live and Die in L.A.*, it was fun to learn to counterfeit money, and that runs deep—I know how to counterfeit money! There's nothing esoteric about it. It's real hands-on experience. If I know how to counterfeit money, then I am a counterfeiter. If you're working with weapons and you know how to use the weapons, it's in your body. The most important thing about preparation is getting the stuff in your body. In *Platoon*, the preparation was very important—to get moving through the jungle in your body. I just do real practical things that have to do with me. I don't think I can be anything other than what I am, but I think in this body, in this mind, there is infinite possibility. It's all about applying what's in this body and mind, my history, to a series of actions. Out of these actions comes a character, and I think action is what defines character.

HAVE YOU STUDIED ACTING AT ALL?

Not really formally. The study has really been *working*, because I've worked a lot. With Theater X, and now with The Wooster Group, I work every day. When I'm not making a film, I'm rehearsing and performing every day. It's really mostly learning by doing. I believe a lot in intuition, and I believe over the years you develop a technique, but it's not articulated. It's not like a problem-solving machine, where if you've got a problem, you just send it through the mill. For me, it's best that way. Training is a curious thing in any profession. You think of a kid who wants to be a doctor when he is 18. He goes through premed, he goes to medical school, he does his internship, he does his residency . . . God, this guy is practically 30 before he's ready to practice. In twelve years, a lot can change. It's hard to track your life. I think acting is much more than a craft. I can really speak some voodoo. It's got huge elements of spirituality to it at its

best. It can also be very whorish and shlocky, but at its best, it is a great meditation. When you do a film or performance, it's almost like a prayer: offering yourself off into this piece of fiction. It's almost like stopping time, stepping out of what you do and saying, "This is a special time, and I am going to behave in such and such a way for this period of time."

WHAT HAS BEEN YOUR BIGGEST SACRIFICE FOR SUCCESS?

I try not to think in those terms. I don't think I've sacrificed anything, and I'm not sure I'm a success.

WHAT IS THE BIGGEST MISCONCEPTION ABOUT YOU?

People think I'm really big when they see me in movies, but I'm only 5'9", 145 lbs. That is actually quite slight for a man.

IS BEING AN ACTOR EVER A STRUGGLE FOR YOU?

It's a terrific struggle because there's no clear lines of, "If you do this, you get that." It's all kind of fractured, and because I work fairly intuitively, I have no technique I can apply my energy to all the time that's kind of fail-safe. Each time out, each performance, each time approaching a project, it's a struggle. You've never been there before—it's new. And just like anything new, it's exciting but it's scary. When you don't field it well, you become angry with yourself. When it doesn't turn out well, there's no particular reason, and if it does, then who says it turned out well? It just is. Once again, the struggle is against effect and reward. Everything with our lives and everything about theater and film flirts with that, but at the same time, you have to abandon that notion to do great things.

WHAT DO YOU LIKE BEST ABOUT SUCCESS?

I like that once you get elevated to a certain profile, people are watching you. I'm interested in my life, and I'm crazy enough to want other people to watch me as I go through the thing. I like being watched. I like company. I don't have a lot of friends and I don't go out a lot, but I'm

basically social and somewhere deeply, I like people to be with me.

DO YOU LIKE BEING WITH YOURSELF?

No. Well, yes I do, but it's like that quote from Pascal, and I wish I could say it exactly, but essentially, he attributes the misery of the whole world to the fact that men essentially can't sit alone in their rooms. Most people search for distractions because, once they're thrown on themselves, they're forced with the great philosophical agonies of being a person.

WHAT IS YOUR BIGGEST FEAR?

I'm afraid of everything a little bit, but I'm not afraid of anything a lot. I flip-flop quite a bit. I'm a steady, stable sort of person, although as I get older, I think I'm more neurotic than I thought I was. I flip-flop between recklessness and great worry.

HOW DO YOU DEAL WITH YOUR FANS?

When I first started getting a lot of fan mail, it really felt bad not to be able to answer it, but I just couldn't practically do it, and I hired someone to do it to some degree. I still feel kind of crummy, but I'm a fool in that way because you can't. It's a dead end to pretend any sort of intimacy with a stranger. It's unfair, because they see you on the screen. I have it myself. I'm not starstruck, but I'll see great work, and I do get curious about the people, and I want to have some sort of contact with them. I understand the impulse; I don't find it frivolous and totally silly. On the street, I hear people out if I have time. If I don't, I don't.

WHICH OF YOUR PEERS DO YOU RESPECT?

I respect the people in the Wooster Group. I see performances I love, but I guess I hesitate to mention particular names because when I see them in print there's something icky about it. Put it this way, I've got no shrine in my bathroom for anyone, and when I go out to a place where I know there's going to be celebrity types, I don't think about meeting anyone in particular.

WHAT TO YOU IS INTUITION?

I keep coming back to the notion of things being effect-oriented, and the whole idea of thinking, you know. People are always trying to say something; I can say something with my life, but I have nothing to say. I can say something in a performance, but there's nothing I want the character to tell people. I think you do things and they create their own sense of truth. They become fact, and then people can do whatever they want with them. Of course I am speaking as a performer, but this idea of shaping something to create a certain effect is foolish. Once you get there, well . . . It's that old story that if you're going to the Grand Canyon and you've got to drive like hell to get there—or you're so determined because you saw a picture of the Grand Canyon, it's set in your head—you're going to be blind for the whole trip, and once you get there, you're not even going to see it. It has something to do with that. I try to feel my way along, and I think that's called intuition. I just trust the feeling of knowing where I am going. I am present-minded, and all that means is being suspicious of any kind of accumulation, to know you are at the mercy of so many different forces, you'd just better know where you are in any given moment. The next step you can deal with when you get there. I think it's pretty simple.

HOW DO YOU FEEL YOU FIT INTO THE CONTEXT *THE NEW BREED*?

It sounds right to me. I don't know too many people like me. I think the way I approach acting may circle around to something else, but I don't feel an affinity for the way most other actors approach their work. I think what we call acting in this country was poisoned by Lee Strasberg's interpretation of Stanislavsky somewhere in the Fifties, and I think it bound up a lot of stuff in a certain kind of realism that is limiting.

SO, BOTTOM LINE, WHY ARE YOU AN ACTOR?

For my own pleasure and to create beauty. I hope people will enjoy what I create.

Patrick Swayze

Patrick Swayze's journey to box-office bankability as one of Hollywood's hottest leading men has been a long, arduous one. He began performing in musical theater as a child in Houston, Texas, and moved to Manhattan to dance with the Eliot Feld Ballet Company. Massive knee injuries forced him to give up ballet, and after trying musical comedy on Broadway, he moved to Los Angeles to pursue a film career.

Patrick performed in a string of films that were critically acclaimed yet commercial bombs (e.g., *The Outsiders*, *Red Dawn*). He was not interested in making movies just to make movies; his choices were grounded in making a statement with each film he made.

The summer sleeper *Dirty Dancing* catapulted Patrick into the limelight, establishing him as a romantic leading man. He's not entirely satisfied with his new status, however, because people treat him differently now, and he feels that once you become a star, people can't see past that.

WHAT WAS THE FIRST THING YOU STARTED DOING IN THE ARTS?

Everything. My mother didn't believe you could truly call yourself an artist unless you were well-rounded in every area of the arts, so I was taking dance classes, playing the violin and doing children's theater for as long as I can remember.

HOW DID OTHER KIDS YOUR AGE REACT TO YOUR INVOLVEMENT WITH THE ARTS?

They'd make fun of me. There was one really bad time when I first went to junior high school: I got beat up really badly by five guys behind the church—but later on I got them back.

HOW DID YOU DO THAT?

When I had recovered from my injuries, my father came with me on my first day back at school and set it up with the head coach so that I could fight these guys one at a time with gloves on. One of them was the school bully. He had failed three or four times; he was 18 in the ninth grade. When we were assembled in the weight

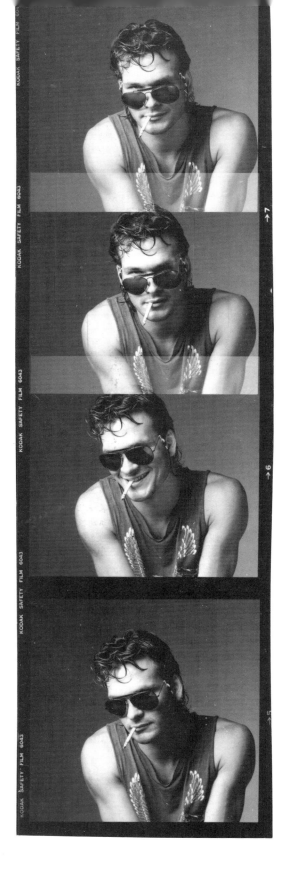

room, the coach handed the gloves to me and to one other guy. My father took both pairs of gloves and tossed them. The coach said, "You can't do that," but my father said, "Watch me. My son is at least going to have the chance one-on-one to do to them what they did to him." It was a real Texas sort of way of dealing with people. I fought all five of them, one at a time, and I beat them all. I thought that would fix things for me because I had beaten the toughest guy in the school, but all it did was make *me* the tough guy, and everyone wanted to fight me after that. That made my life a little bit more miserable.

I got a chance to learn some big lessons early though. At 13, I decided to quit dancing so that people would leave me alone. It didn't work; it didn't change a thing. I then realized something very important: Screw the world or anybody who tries to make me believe something different than what I believe, or tell me that my dreams can't come true. I've never let anybody ever stop me again from achieving what I want to achieve.

WHAT WAS THE DIFFERENCE BETWEEN DANCING WITH A BALLET COMPANY AND PERFORMING IN A BROADWAY MUSICAL?

Because I had discipline drilled into me from the time I can remember, it was a fairly painless transition. I understood what it took to be good on the level it required, and I was willing to do that. If anything, it's become something I live my life by.

SO DISCIPLINE IS STILL VERY IMPORTANT TO YOU?

Very much. Early on in Hollywood, I'd walk into offices and there were 30 other clones sitting there; I knew I was going to blow them away. I had that confidence because I had done the work, and I *knew* I'd done the work. I never stopped studying; I never stopped continuing to grow. That was the one thing that always pulled me through. I just found that looking into most of those other guys' eyes, that's as deep as you could see. They were just interested in getting out there and seeing how far they could get by on their looks and personality.

WHAT IS THE HARDEST THING ABOUT ACTING FOR YOU?

Character studies; I find that they are the scariest things I have ever attempted in my life. Because my function, my responsibility as an actor is to break down my barriers, my defenses and the things I put up to insulate myself from the pain of the world—yet somehow I still have to protect myself. It's very contradictory. I find the longer I go, the deeper I go inside my myself, these dark recesses and corners—Pandora's Box. You open that and start looking in it, and it's very, very scary. What you ultimately wind up doing is psychoanalyzing yourself—which can be dangerous if not handled correctly.

AND HOW DO YOU HANDLE IT CORRECTLY?

Instinct. I still have a lot of life ahead of me to see if I am successful in it; it remains to be seen. At this moment in life, I feel I'm walking a dangerous line—that place where there's a great deal of fear coming up when I do a character. I'm attracted to very intense characters, so that hypes the potential power of a performance and the potential emotional damage.

I'm just trying to sort out what all of this success means, and trying to stay clear with my ideals and my integrity, and not get sucked into what happens to so many people who become subject to this imitation of life in Hollywood. It's not an easy thing, because the machine is set up to suck you in. If you do get sucked in, it's death as an actor.

HOW DO YOU AVOID GETTING SUCKED IN?

Right now I'm trying to remember exactly why I'm doing this. I feel you have to have a purpose in your life—you have to have something bigger than yourself in order to keep your head on your shoulders. I've lived my life up to this point with a desire to make a contribution through my work, and to affect people's lives in a positive way through my work and through doing press. That's why I take press very seriously. I feel I have a responsibility to do that, to return something—not to be a bloodsucker. It's also a self-preservation because it keeps you out of your ego and keeps your feet on the ground.

ARE YOU CONTINUING TO STUDY?

Yeah. But I haven't gone back to class; I haven't had much time. I've literally been doing movie after movie for eight years now. What happened as a result of that is that I've lost that purpose in my life—I've lost the passion. I wind up having to talk about that passion and my ideals and my beliefs to journalist nonstop until it almost sounds like bullshit instead of something I truly believe. I'm trying to rediscover that purpose and get the passion back.

DO YOU FEEL YOU'VE GIVEN EVERYTHING AWAY AND HAVEN'T KEPT ANYTHING FOR YOURSELF?

Yes. I'm just fighting emptiness—fighting this pit in my insides that I can't get rid of. It's been coming on for a few years now. I'm so accustomed to putting on the armor in the battle act, picking up my battle axes, going into the fray and trying to do quality work; I don't even know how to recognize or deal with a supportive situation anymore. It's hard when everyone else around you is trying to get you to sell out.

HOW DO YOU FEEL ABOUT THE MAJORITY OF SCRIPTS YOU ARE SUBMITTED?

The quality has drastically changed—or should I say the quantity? You work so hard to get to this place in your life, and then you get there, you find it doesn't really change anything. You're offered a lot more scripts and you get a chance at the "A" projects, but you realize there are so few good scripts out there that it makes you sick. So what I'm doing now is creating my own projects.

WHAT DO YOU LOOK FOR IN A SCRIPT?

Power and passion. Can I affect people's lives or make their lives lighter for a moment, or make them understand something better through what I do?

WHEN YOU TAKE A PART, DO YOU CONSIDER WHAT EFFECT THE FILM WILL HAVE ON PEOPLE?

Very much so. Everybody saw *Red Dawn* as a film about right-wing fascism. I saw something completely different in the role of Jed. I saw an opportunity to make an incredible antiwar statement by having

people see the destruction on your soul by warlike attitudes. Adults and critics didn't get that, but the film has a cult following all over the world; the kids got it—the youth got it—and that makes me feel wonderful.

WHAT SOCIAL ISSUES ARE IMPORTANT TO YOU?

I think something has happened to the world, or at least to the United States—apathy, and people feeling completely ineffectual and powerless. I want to try, in whatever way I can, to help restore that power in people. I don't have the answers to the world; I only know what *I* need to fix and work for myself. But I've found that the problems I'm having seem to be the problems the world is having.

WHAT ARE YOU DOING TO MAKE A DIFFERENCE?

Through press, the things I talk about and the roles I choose. *Dirty Dancing* was a sweet little film, but I had a very specific point I wanted to bring off about class structure and social prejudice. I also wanted to bring dancing back to a form of communication and connection with another human being—not swing your butt on the dance floor in a bar so maybe you'll get picked up. My focus is to get myself back to a true level of communication with other people, and to help myself and other men try to find out what being a man means these days. I think my father's generation was doomed. Their upbringing was such that men were to act one way and women were to act another way. Now, men are required to be real, feeling, vulnerable human beings. I think we have a chance to fight our prior training, and our children will have more of a chance. I've done some bad-ass characters, but what I try to do is bring to them a level of vulnerability and sensitivity to create that something that is sought after rather than feared.

WHEN YOU GET A PART, HOW DO YOU APPROACH A ROLE AND WHAT KIND OF PREPARATION DO YOU DO?

I do as much literal and physical research as necessary, but my biggest focus is where my character comes from and what his history is. I write a whole scenario about his life—what kind of parents he had, what kind of car he drives, what kinds of problems he has and how they manifest themselves physically in terms of quirks. Your character is revealed by how you *conceal* the emotion. Your whole key as an actor is the ability to conceal emotion—letting the audience see by what you're trying to cover up, what he really wants.

WHAT HAS BEEN YOUR BIGGEST SACRIFICE FOR SUCCESS?

I'm normally a very outgoing person, and I'm finding I'm having to become more reserved and more reclusive; the loneliness is intense even in my personal relationships. I'm being hit from all sides and then some, and I've got to protect myself. The world wants to see you as this and that. I read this *Newsweek* article about me that blew me away.

ABOUT WHAT?

It's about a cult that's developing around Johnny Castleman from *Dirty Dancing*. These women are starting a club for women who love Patrick Swayze too much. It's very weird.

HOW DO YOU DEAL WITH THAT?

I just try to continue with things that my wife Lisa and I started. Our life is here on the ranch, training horses and tending to our animals and each other, while trying to move forward and create some kind of quality in our lives.

ARE YOUR FEELINGS OF LONELINESS AND EMPTINESS A RESULT OF THE WALL YOU'VE HAD TO BUILD AROUND YOURSELF BECAUSE OF SUCCESS?

Yeah, but that wall is in direct opposition to my key as an actor. I can't let that wall build up—I can't. If I let that wall build up, do you realize how much power as a human being I'm leaving behind?

ARE YOU TRYING TO FIND THAT MIDDLE GROUND RIGHT NOW?

Exactly, and it's not an easy one to find. It's not easy not to believe the hype when *everybody* is expecting you to believe it. "Well, how does it feel to be a sex symbol?" "How does it feel for women to be

screaming and going crazy for you?" That kind of thing. I have to put it in some sort of real perspective. In Germany and Norway, I had ten bodyguards nonstop. It's weird to be standing insulated by these bodies, and all these people are trying to get at you, screaming and crying. I realized something in that moment: I'm only a catalyst, as is any rock star or movie star or anyone who is publicly idolized. You are only a catalyst for these people to release something, because, God, I saw panic I saw need in these eyes to get something out. I'm realizing now they're not really screaming for me—I'm just affording them an opportunity. That made me feel proud in that moment. It made me feel like there was a purpose to this lunacy.

IS BEING AN ACTOR A STRUGGLE FOR YOU?

Yeah, but as much as I talk about the fear and needing to sort it all out, right now is the most exciting challenge I've ever had in my life. As an actor, a dancer and a songwriter, my creative possibilities are infinite. There's so much room to grow.

DO YOU BELIEVE WHAT YOUR MOTHER INSTILLED IN YOU AS A CHILD, THAT IN ORDER TO BE A TRUE ARTIST YOU HAVE TO BE WELL-ROUNDED?

Absolutely. When I went to New York to dance, I knew I never would be Baryshnikov on a technical level. What I knew how to do, however, was allow my emotional life to move through my body so I could affect people. It became more of a giving rather than, "Oh, watch me."

IF YOU COULD STAR IN AN ON SCREEN BIOGRAPHY OF SOMEONE, WHO WOULD IT BE AND WHY?

I'd like to play Jim Morrison. I know Travolta has always wanted to do it—he's pushed and pushed to try to get that role—but there are too many legal problems right now. I'd like to do it for many reasons. I don't believe Morrison was a god, like many people think; I believe he copped out and ran away. I'd like to play him from a realistic point of view—this man was driven crazy by his own soul. If I could play Jim Morrison, I think I could

blow people away. I'm trying to sort that out for myself in life, and I'd love to do that sort of character onscreen.

WHAT SPIRITUAL THINGS ARE IMPORTANT TO YOU?

To continue to find my center. In martial arts you call it finding your *ki*. I live my life for those moments as an actor, a dancer and a singer, because it's in those moments that you have an innate organic understanding of how you fit into this world, in this life and in this universe. I've found in martial arts a wonderful release—a connection. When you've truly found you *ki*, it's amazing. The terrible part is, when you're fighting, trying to achieve this level of finding your center, once you've hit it, everything will go into slow motion. Fighting one, two, three guys becomes child's play. It is beautiful, this incredible feeling, but then you look at the results, the *effect* of what you've done—the reality that you've destroyed someone's face.

BUT CAN'T YOU USE THIS ENERGY IN A DIFFERENT WAY?

Exactly. That's why I act. I live for those moments when I fly with a role and achieve my *ki*. It may only happen one or two times in a whole film, though.

HOW DO YOU FEEL YOU FIT INTO THE CONTEXT OF THE NEW BREED?

The new breed is focused on going past where other people have gone before. Acting styles are different than they used to be—they're completely based on reality now, and that's not to put a quality judgment on actors of the past. The new breed in many ways are trying to sort out their own lives through the roles they do. It's a catharsis for the world to see.

It's really interesting where things are going in this world. Alarms are going off in my insides big-time because I think things are real, real dangerous now; it all has to do with that lethargic attitude about life. People are screaming, screaming to find a group, to find a religion, to find something, to have some sort of harmony with other people. My purpose as an actor, and as part of the new breed, is to help form that harmony.

Sean Young

"Acting kills me. Dead. My heart stops once I know I have a role. When I read *The Boost* screenplay, I had to get a beer and a cigarette just to sit down to stop for a second to read it. I don't know why I was shaking before I sat down to read the script, but I was shaking. Suddenly I dread the awesome responsibility." My name is Linda. Linda Brown."

**From *Dancing In the Woods*
A diary by Sean Young
August 1987**

HAVE YOU ALWAYS WRITTEN IN A JOURNAL?

I've written in a journal since I was 13. A lot of people who work with me ask me how I stay so sane, so together. I really feel the only reason I do is because I've written in a journal for so long, and I have somebody to turn to who always wants to listen to me, so I never feel alone. It's a very healthy process for me. When I started *The Boost* [co-starring James Woods, in which Sean ends up a battered wife] I wanted to see if I could write a journal in the same way Tony Bentley wrote *A Winter Season* for the ballet—it was honest and so immediate. I wanted to see if I could create that and give people the feeling of what it would be like to experience making a movie. Now that it's done, I don't know if I will publish it.

Movies are kind of a cosmic experience for the person that goes through them—you have to face the fears of your character, whether you want to or not. That's the hard part. It's not technical—it's your heart and soul. You give blood.

WHEN DID YOU DECIDE YOU WANTED TO BECOME AN ACTRESS?

When I got the job. I went to Interlochan Arts Academy for eleventh and twelfth grade. I didn't fit into normal high school—I was afraid of people and they were afraid of me—so my parents sent me to boarding school. It was the first school I was happy in, because I got to

study dance, art, drama and writing. I was in an environment that could support my needs, and since I was away from home, I got to take care of myself and experience life as an individual. After I graduated, I went to New York City and started studying at the School Of American Ballet. But after a summer of that, I quit—I realized I didn't have the right personality for being a ballerina. It wasn't very humorous; it's very hard work and very little pay, and much like the army, where you have to work up through the ranks. Then you don't even have a long career. I'll never know whether I could have been Patricia McBride; I think I could have been, but I didn't like the pain.

Then I became a model. I was with Zoli, and I did that for about a year; then I quit that, too. I didn't like it at all. Nothing I considered to be *really* me was being asked of; nothing I had to offer inside, was being taken advantage of. The working conditions were really difficult for me as an individual, as a personality. I had trouble watching the other models I was working with and how unhappy they were. I knew *that* wasn't what I wanted.

My mom introduced me to an agent at ICM. A month after I signed with them, I auditioned for James Ivory and got a role in *Jane Austen in Manhattan*. After that I got *Stripes*, and since then I've just been in the right place at the right time, and I've gotten hired. I've been shooting film after film, back to back.

WHAT WERE YOUR GOALS WHEN YOU FIRST STARTED OUT AND HOW HAVE THEY CHANGED?

My goals when I first started out in terms of moviemaking was just to be able to show up on time and be cooperative—to try to listen to what it was that the director was telling me to do. While shooting *Young Doctors in Love*, however, I realized I had listened to what everyone else had been telling me, but I hadn't gotten the best out of myself—I was leaving that in the hands of everyone else. Suddenly at 23, I realized that I had to develop an opinion about my work, and that I had to become responsible for whatever image I was projecting on the screen. I felt the best way to become responsible, in terms of my work, was to become responsible in terms of my *life*—and that meant to come home, get an apartment, pay bills, settle in and keep it running. Now my goals are

to understand the material, to understand *who* I'm playing and how she fits into the grand scheme of things, what the character teaches me.

HOW DO YOU FEEL ABOUT THE MAJORITY OF SCRIPTS YOU ARE SUBMITTED?

Most scripts are fairly poor; I think that's well-known throughout the industry. If you want to do good work, you have to choose good material, and if you're going to do that, you're going to have to work less. I would love to just do little tiny parts here and there, like I did in *Wall Street*, because it's fun and the pressure isn't as rough as a lead role. Lead roles make me grow up, which I am afraid of doing.

WHAT DO YOU LOOK FOR IN A SCRIPT?

I look for parts where the female character is well-defined. I'm practical—like, will I have to swim, ride a horse or climb a cliff? I don't like scripts that force me to be uncomfortable. I've done enough of those things to know I don't want to do them anymore. I don't want to have to take my clothes off for every movie. It didn't bother me in this last movie [*The Boost*], because it was a great film, but I don't like it and don't want anymore men pawing my body from now on.

BUT YOU WANT TO AVOID SUPERCILIOUS NUDITY?

Exactly. I've been in situations where I was forced to comply if I wanted to further my career, and I was able to do it, but it's not the greatest feeling. *No Way Out*'s nudity is supercilious, but I knew *that* film was my chance to score in terms of a cinema presence—it was a bombshell part. If you are smart enough and intellectual enough, you can take a part further and do more than what's written there. I knew what was there for me with *No Way Out*.

When you're a dancer, you're used to dealing with your body in a detached way, so I don't have any difficulty with that. Most people wonder how I do it so easily; the hardest part is going to the screening with my mother. I do it because I'm trying to balance my career and take advantage of opportunities. I look at scripts now, and if I have to be mauled, naked, or have these ridiculous non-ending pan shots from the butt to the breast to the head, I just toss it.

YOU'VE DONE QUITE A FEW FILMS WITH A LOT OF SPECIAL EFFECTS—*DUNE, BLADERUNNER* AND *BABY*; WHICH WAS THE MOST DIFFICULT TO MAKE?

Dune. I had to wear this still suit made out of rubber, and it was the summer in the desert, so it was very uncomfortable. Plus my role was of a Fremen, so every time I had a closeup, they put a sandbag in front of a fan and shook it—so dust was flying in my face all day.

WHAT KIND OF ROLES ARE YOU LOOKING FOR?

Comedy—that's what I'm best at; that's the area I've been exposed the least. I think it's because I can be dramatic and people tend to jump on that ability. In *The Boost*, I did such a dramatic role—a lot of crying, a lot of pain. When someone sees that, their first thought is not going to be, "Wow, what a great comedienne."

I have the feeling that my roles choose *me*; I don't really choose my roles. I didn't choose *Bladerunner*. [Sean played Harrison Ford's android love interest.] Ridley Scott just saw me and decided he knew what he could do with me, so I got the part. The scariest thing is when you know a role is perfect for you, and you look at everything that it's going to put you through. I have to seriously consider whether I can handle it.

IS STUDYING IMPORTANT FOR YOUR GROWTH AS AN ACTRESS?

Yeah. I don't study while in Los Angeles. New York City is my home, and it's where I go to return to my studies. It's an environment I'm very happy in, and very anonymous in. I'm not a movie star in New York, and in that way I remain very centered and happy. People never recognize me walking down the street. It's great and I love it. There are times when I dress up and go out in New York, and I play "Sean Young the movie star." It's definitely an acting part.

WHAT IS THE DIFFERENCE BETWEEN YOU AND YOUR ONSCREEN IMAGE?

I'm very quiet and reclusive, and I like to read and to write, and grow plants. People often come up to me and say, "I love you, you're so wonderful," but what they're really responding to is Sean Young plus what the camera does to her, and the camera *does* do something to me—it really changes the way I look. I often feel when I'm in front of the camera that I'm being added to by a higher force, and that's not voodoo talk. That's just what I feel is happening. People are responding to the added-to version of me. It wouldn't be easy for me to explain to them that me alone is an entirely different person. The makeup people are always amazed at how different I am after putting on the makeup, putting on the hair, putting on the costume, getting in front of lights and putting the camera on. That is where my work begins; that is when my work happens—in the photograph. When I was little, they called me "Sean, Sean the leprechaun," and it's true.

WHAT HAS BEEN YOUR BIGGEST SACRIFICE FOR SUCCESS?

The insanity of the whirlwind that comes over me when I'm making a part. It's not really a sacrifice; it's more like a challenge: Can I remain whole as I go through this? Can I remain kind? Can I remain together? It's hard. Also, I'm a very home-oriented person, so every time I have to work, I always consider leaving home a big sacrifice.

IS BEING AN ACTRESS EVER A STRUGGLE FOR YOU?

Yes & No. Working is easy, but afterward, recovering myself is hard.

WHAT DO YOU LIKE BEST ABOUT SUCCESS?

The money and the freedom money gives you—there's no other reason to do it. There's no gratification in your life being everybody else's fantasy. Maybe some people are into that, but I'm not. Madonna and Sean Penn must suffer so much, because their personal life is so much a part of everybody else's business. I feel lucky because nobody seems to know anything about me; nobody seems to invade me that way.

WHAT HAS BEEN YOUR BIGGEST DISAPPOINTMENT UP TO THIS POINT?

I'm not into disappointments. When you have disappointments, you are creating them. I really do believe that we are responsible for our lives—and if you have a lot of disappointments, you're setting yourself up for them and you're creating them. I've had days when I worked so

hard I woke up crying, thinking, "I can't do this much longer, but I just have to keep my focus." Moviemaking is very difficult; it's not that glamorous. I can say that I don't have any disappointments, because I got into the movie business clean and I've been able to work steadily and not take any waitressing jobs.

IF YOU COULD STAR IN AN ONSCREEN BIOGRAPHY, WHO WOULD IT BE AND WHY?

I would like to portray my great–great grandmother. She grew up in Louisville, Kentucky, and she was married to a man who was in the civil war. When her husband caught malaria, she asked for permission from the Confederate government to go to him in Vicksburg. When she got there, he was dead. It's the story of a woman who got her slaves into a wagon, traveled across Confederate land to her husband and was intent on saving his life. At that time, for a woman to do that was pretty brave. I would like to play her.

WHAT SPIRITUAL THINGS ARE IMPORTANT TO YOU?

Meditating and reading the Bible. My mantra is "Ma-Ra-Na-Tha." It means, "The Lord is present." It's the language Christ spoke in. I got confirmed in 1985, and my priest taught that to me. He's into Christian meditation—it's a new idea.

DID YOU HAVE A BORN-AGAIN EXPERIENCE?

I don't really know what "born-again" means. I just know that because I didn't grow up with the guilt of Catholicism, I can appreciate the *truth* of it, and not play into the hands of sinning and damnation ideas. I think Catholicism has been confused throughout the centuries; it has caused so much pain and has been interpreted so many different ways that there's a lot of room for people to be turned off to Jesus because of it.

To me, the whole point of it is that God is within you, and the temple of life is within you. That's very similar to Buddhism, but I don't feel I have to pay any attention to limitations. I can take the best out of what I believe for myself.

DO YOU THINK THERE IS A SHORTAGE OF GOOD ROLES FOR WOMEN IN HOLLYWOOD TODAY?

I think there's always a shortage of female parts.

WHY DO YOU THINK THERE ARE NO LEADING LADIES TODAY, LIKE JOAN CRAWFORD, KATHARINE HEPBURN, BETTE DAVIS, ETC., OF YESTERDAY'S HOLLYWOOD"

Because of the excessive attention our culture places on the masculine, we have a situation where men are more highly valued and paid better. There's no sense complaining about it, though. As a woman, all you can do is do the best work you know how to do, and maybe your presence on film will be valued and maybe you will make some sort of impression and will have the same kind of stature Robert Redford has. You can't hold your breath for it, either, which is why I like to continue with my own personal activities—they give my life pleasure.

WHO IS THE IDEAL LEADING MAN YOU COULD BE CAST OPPOSITE?

I'd like to work with Jack Nicholson, Dustin Hoffman, Sean Penn . . . —I'd like to work with Kyle MacLachlan again; he's wonderful—he bakes bread. If I could have it my way, I'd like to be the star of a movie and choose the male lead from the new ranks; that would be the most exciting thing. There are a lot of great new young actors; all you have to do is look around and you'll see a lot of talent out there. I'd like to be in a position to help cast them and start someone else's career.

WHAT SOCIAL ISSUES ARE IMPORTANT TO YOU?

Children. I give money and time to a couple of charity organizations; the Covenant House in N.Y.C., Thursday's Child is one of them, The Christian Children's Crusade is another. I just feel the children are our future, and we have to take care of them and give them as much as possible.

HOW DO YOU FEEL YOU FIT INTO THE CONTEXT OF THE NEW BREED?

I mean, I think it's pretty new-wave to be a movie star and have nobody recognize you! It's pretty new-wave to be able to sew dresses and paint and write, like a renaissance woman. I feel being able to express myself is the most important thing in my life; all that, and to stay close to God at the same time.

P.S. Sean quit smoking New Years Eve 1987

Robert Downey, Jr.

At 18, Robert Downey, Jr. found himself out on his own. Financial ties severed by his father, the avant-garde director of such films as *Putney Swope*, Robert was forced to fend for himself, but he wasn't worried—he was a survivor. The only hunger he was unable to satisfy, however, was his intense appetite for drugs and alcohol.

Drugs have always played a major role in Robert's life, though recently he has begun to come to terms with his past and himself, deciding that his new outlook on life is better off without them. Acting allows him the possibility to get more in touch with his feelings every day. Through his work, Robert wishes to expose the duplicity of the world in which we live. The real world is not the one we always perceive, rather there is a deeper reality. It is this undisguised reality that Robert concerns himself with showing.

WHY WAS IT SO TOUGH?

A lot of it had to do with growing up in a family where everyone was doing drugs and trying to be creative—there was always a lot of pot and coke around. It wasn't like my dad was such a drug addict; drugs became an excuse for him to do his writing, or his writing became an excuse to do drugs. When my dad and I would do drugs together, it was like him trying to express his love for me in the only way he knew how.

HOW OLD WERE YOU WHEN YOU FIRST DID DRUGS TOGETHER?

Eight. To me, it always seemed like a staple in life. It was cool, but I *never* felt like any other fucking kid in my school.

SO YOU MOVED AROUND A LOT?

Always. I say this jokingly, but it seems kinda right: Whenever I'd tell Dad I met someone or made a good friend, he'd say, "Pack your bags—we're leaving."

WHAT HAPPENED WHEN YOUR PARENTS GOT DIVORCED?

Well, they had been together for 15 years and they were partners more than husband and wife; there was a great sense of humor and irony in their relationship. For whatever reasons, nothing is one-sided— things broke up and she was more shell-shocked than anyone else in the family. My sister went with my dad, for reasons only she knows. She was the one they had sent to private school and thought was going to do great things. I was this weird pothead kid who got off blowing away frogs with my BB gun. I went with my mom because she needed me.

SO WHERE DID YOU AND YOUR MOM MOVE TO?

We moved to 19 E. 48th Street between Madison and 5th. It was a five-floor walkup to this depressing fucking place with no windows . . . well, there were windows but there were bars in them and there was always this grainy gray light coming through them. It always seemed like it was 6:00 p.m. I can't relate to real poverty, but we were cooking on a burner instead of an oven, and we were trying to create this sense of family or happiness in the skankiest of surroundings. I didn't spend much time there; I was out with the boys, hanging out in Washington Square, going to *The Rocky Horror Picture Show*, doing whippits and intermittently stopping back in the house to steal most of Mom's cash. I think just the fact I was there for her was kinda enough, in a way.

SO WHEN DID YOU DECIDE TO BECOME AN ACTOR?

I did this play about SMU called "Fraternity," and it wasn't so much that I decided to become an actor as it was that acting was something good for me to do, something I *wanted* to do. Most of the things in my life were pursued out of necessity, not out of desire. I had this extreme paranoia that led me to be good. I was so afraid of not having my shit together, I'd get to the theater an hour and a half before every show, stretch out on this mat and run over actions and transitions in my head. This paranoia gave me discipline. The other guys would come in and say, "Downey's gone to Nirvana again."

What's weird is that, at that time in my life, I was also just getting into spiritual stuff—like the human energy systems, auras and projections of consciousness. I felt like it wasn't even me going out to get all of these books—it was my higher self saying, "Fuck, this kid's in trouble; we better surround him with a lot of good thoughts."

WERE YOU IN TROUBLE BECAUSE OF SUBSTANCE ABUSE?

Yeah. It's so much easier to spend every night out getting drunk with the boys and making a thousand phone calls in pursuit of drugs than to stop and say, "OK, what am I going to do tomorrow when I wake up late, and it all just starts over again?" Substance abuse is just a real easy way to give yourself something to do every day. It's something you know you always get the same result from, not trying something different like changing your life—you don't know what the results are going to be then, success or failure. I've never *failed* to get high from smoking a joint; I've never failed to get depressed from doing coke. Even though there are usually negative outcomes, at least you know it's going to be that same fucking negative every time, and it's so comfortable.

Now I'm into sobriety by default. I've beat a fucking dead horse for three years—quitting, slipping and quitting again. It's enough. I kept it up until fairly recently, but now it's time to move on. *Less Than Zero* was sort of a catharsis for me, except the difference between Julian and me is that Julian had a death wish—he just wanted to die. Maybe I've ridden that fucking line between life and death desperately, without a net, but if I had gotten into basing, I'd be dead now. I know my limitations, I know I'm excessive and I know I'm not going to kill myself.

WHAT WERE YOUR GOALS WHEN YOUR FIRST STARTED OUT AND HOW HAVE THEY CHANGED?

My goals at first were all material and external—a million dollars, my name above titles, everyone knowing who I am and all my friends saying, "I wish I was him." I didn't think I'd be any happier, but at least I'd have the guise of success. Now my goals are more internal; they still have to do with the business I'm in, but they are to make myself happy and whole. Acting really helps—it gives me a focus and lets me express stuff that maybe I can relay to other people.

CAN YOU BE MORE SPECIFIC AS TO WHAT YOU MEAN BY INTERNAL GOALS?

I don't really think we live in the "real" world. I keep having flashes of what I think reality is, which is the simultaneous nature of time and the energy behind all matter; we're all from that reservoir. That's why when I hear people say, "Downey has such screen presence," I know all they're seeing is the reality of the spirit behind the

matter. I feel that what's really home is not my body, my car or anything I can really touch, it's the things with the inner senses. I think that's where I—and *everyone*—has the most work to do. That's why I like sleeping so much—I really know where I am when I'm sleeping. Even If I don't remember it when I wake up, I'm home when I'm sleeping.

HOW DO YOU FEEL ABOUT MOST OF THE SCRIPTS YOU ARE SUBMITTED?

It makes me so fucking angry. Where have we come if in the 1980s, hopefully the beginning of the Golden Age, all the scripts are about guns and dicks? It's sort of entertainment, but nothing really happens. It's so geared toward violence, self-indulgence and mindless comedy, without any intellectual backup.

WHAT DO YOU LOOK FOR IN A SCRIPT?

It's too easy for me to keep picking scripts that are very me and easy to do, so now I look for roles I wouldn't think I could play right off the bat. I'm looking for something I know I'm going to have to trust myself and expand to do. It really comes down to, "Is this script going to teach me something new about myself?"

SO ARE YOU LOOKING FOR ROLES IN WHICH YOU CAN WORK THINGS OUT IN YOUR OWN LIFE ONSCREEN?

I think so, but Hollywood isn't ready for the kind of films I *really* want to do. I want to do films about spirituality and what's really going on in the undercurrent of this majestic reality everyone is trying to suffocate and not confront. I want to do films where people discover themselves in ways that would be great to shoot. I'm trying to get the rights to a book about this guy going to school in Berkeley who encounters a warrior [from another plane of reality]. The warrior had sought him out because he knew this guy was meant to write a book. The guy was a world-class gymnast; he had everything, yet he had nothing. I want to do films that will move people without being preachy, that will offer one man's means to an end that will give you peace.

WHAT IS THE FOUNDATION OF YOUR SPIRITUALITY?

It's nothing I can articulate, and that's why it makes sense to *me*. It's nothing verbal that I could express as joy or bliss. Spirituality is different for everyone, yet there is a common thread that everyone is within everyone else—we're all the same.

HOW DO YOU APPROACH AND PREPARE FOR A ROLE?

It's different every time. For *Less Than Zero*, I thought about aspects of myself and some of my friends. I said, "Look, this role is an exaggerated version of you, and it's also not you at all, so don't think about it, just do it." For *1969*, I examined the social climate of the time by reading and talking to my dad. No matter how much you research a period piece, you're going to have to make up your own fucking mind about it. Everyone's experience is so varied, yet valid; you're always playing different aspects of yourself anyway. Even if it takes place over ten years, it's two fucking hours—no one can express more than a portion of themselves in a film anyway, and by themselves, I mean *selves*, plural. Right now I'm just experimenting with different things, but who knows what's gonna work?

IS STUDYING IMPORTANT FOR YOUR GROWTH AS AN ACTOR?

I'd love to eventually study with a teacher named Sandra Sekat; from what I get about her, she teaches people about people. Most of the other teachers, I feel, are people who never made it in the industry themselves and are giving people steadfast rules of what they should do. To me, that's bullshit, and they can suck my dick. I don't think that's valid; I don't think someone should impose their beliefs on you, when in the back of their beliefs is their insecurity from not having been successful themselves—or at least successful in the commercial or public eye. Maybe it's me being a snob, but I don't think I have anything to learn from someone who hasn't made it himself.

WOULD YOU DO A NUDE SCENE?

Sure. You can expose yourself a lot more than taking your clothes off. What it would come down to is me saying, "I hope I don't get a hard-on—it would be distracting to the crew and I'd be embarrassed because, shit, maybe it's not as big as I want it to be." My fears about acting are a lot more than showing my physical body; it's about what I might learn about myself so that I'm *really* showing something.

WHEN YOU TAKE A PART, DO YOU CONSIDER WHAT EFFECT THE FILM WILL HAVE ON YOUR PEERS?

I do more lately. I'm not worrying about money, so my struggle is about accomplishing my goals. I was in Georgia, and this lady came up to me shaking and said, "I saw you in *Less Than Zero*." I felt like saying, "Why are you shaking? You're every bit as special as I am," but I was in a pissed-off mood and I didn't want to be a prick, so I said my usual thanks a lot, and started to walk away. Then she said, "Two of my friends went into rehab after seeing you in that movie." I got chills up and down my spine and thought, "Fuck, now I know why I do what I do."

IS BEING AN ACTOR A STRUGGLE FOR YOU?

There's moments of struggle within it, but I'm still searching for a steadfast way to satisfy myself and communicate myself 100%. It will take a catalyst, which is me or someone else, to make that happen. I'm still a foetus. I know so little, but I don't want to keep reinforcing that belief, even though I know it to be true at this moment. Maybe it's about the childish approach I take to what I do, which is the thing that will keep me honest.

WHAT IS THE DIFFERENCE BETWEEN YOU AND YOUR ONSCREEN IMAGE?

My image is of a guy who's always glib, never thinks about anything, has a good sense of humor, does crazy things and doesn't think about the repercussions. Only Sarah [Jessica Parker, his girlfriend], my family and a few good friends—people I really dig—see me. Maybe it unavoidable, but maybe it's something I don't want to share with everyone. There's the Robert Downey who walks out the fucking door into a club or Tower Video, fucking around or trying to act like the happy, nice guy, and then there's the side of me that sits home, reads and is quiet. It pisses me off when people say they know me better than the people who *really* know me. Everyone wants to feel like they're in touch with someone, and it's a great conversation piece, but me—the real me—is someone sacred only a very few people know.

WHAT HAS BEEN YOUR BIGGEST SACRIFICE FOR SUCCESS?

Losing touch with the day-to-day reality of a modest existence. Los Angeles isn't reality, and making a movie that's being put together in Los Angeles is a double entendre of nonreality. What could be sacrificed, but hasn't been yet, is my selfhood and losing touch with Robert. I never get to spend any time alone anymore, and that's got to change. I need time to recharge my batteries.

WHAT IS YOUR BIGGEST FEAR?

Mediocrity. I'm not really afraid of total failure, because I don't think that will happen. I'm not afraid of success, because that beats the hell out of failure. It's being in the *middle* that scares me. I've done some mediocre stuff, and it really bothers me. Having to live with mediocrity is pretty scary.

IF TWO OTHER ACTORS WERE UP FOR THE SAME PART AS YOU, ALL THREE OF YOU WERE EQUAL IN TERMS OF LOOKS, TALENT, ETC., WHY SHOULD A DIRECTOR CHOOSE YOU FOR THE PART OVER THE OTHER TWO ACTORS?

I think I have less fear than any other actor I see working; I'll try anything. Guys turned down reading the part of Julian because they said, "I don't want to play no crack faggot"; I said, "I'll suck cock for base money." I have no fear. I'm also the most fun to hang out with. Fuck the work—the director's going to have to deal with me for six weeks *between* takes. We'd rock whatever town we were shooting in.

HOW DO YOU FEEL YOU FIT INTO THE CONTEXT OF THE NEW BREED?

The new breed is youth-oriented. A lot of veterans wouldn't have made it if they had to start their careers today. It's a whole new age of filmmaking and art forms. With the youth getting more control, we're becoming a lot more aware of the world we're living in. Right now I've started to work on Downey, then I'll work my way up to L.A., the United States and maybe, eventually, the planet.

Mary Stuart Masterson

Mary Stuart Masterson was so afraid of failure, she almost didn't become an actress. Growing up in Manhattan's Upper West Side in a creative household (her father is writer/director Peter Masterson and her mother is actress Carlyn Glynn), Mary Stuart says she was extremely insecure. Having hard-working parents with very high ideals she found trying new things difficult. She felt that she had to be perfect, but there was no way she could live up to her self-imposed expectations. She had to learn that it was OK to make mistakes.

It wasn't until doing Horton Foote's play "Lily Dale" off-Broadway that Mary Stuart discovered her self-worth as an actress. Through the process of rehearsals and preparation, she began to accept the validity of her own choices, and she realized that her performances were not simply based on luck.

Her goal is to do roles that truly inspire her on some level; at some point, she also wants to direct, produce and write. Mary Stuart is now allowing herself to learn and grow from her mistakes, and she no longer punishes herself for "not being Meryl Streep yet."

WHAT WAS IT LIKE TO GROW UP IN MANHATTAN?

I grew up in this twelve-story building with six apartments on each floor. The building always smelled of burning cabbage and really smelly pot roast and meat loaf; I guess that's why I'm a vegetarian. Every day I'd walk the dog and this man who smelled of whiskey would walk up to me and flash me and I'd laugh at him. I was only six or seven, but I thought that was kind of funny. I used to wake up at 6:00 a.m. and put on Carly Simon and run around dancing with this great old dog we had named Friendly. He was my best friend.

I used to play in this place we called "the dirt park." The ground was all dirt there, but New York dirt isn't like soil; it smells kind of musty. I used to play war there. It was the boys against the girls, but I would always be on the boy's team.

WERE YOU A TOMBOY?

No, I really wasn't. I was more a flirt than a tomboy, but I knew how to flirt, and I didn't flirt like the other girls did. I flirted by knowing the boys better, understanding them and joking with them. I knew they appreciated that more than girls flipping their hair and giggling a lot; they couldn't stand that and neither could I.

IF I WERE TO ASK YOUR FRIENDS FROM HIGH SCHOOL WHAT YOU WERE LIKE, WHAT WOULD THEY SAY AND HOW WOULD THEY DESCRIBE YOU?

I went to a private school called Dalton. My first day I walked into my English class and Jenny Lumet, who turned out to be my best friend in high school, says I was wearing a baby-blue sweatshirt, baby-blue cords and I had ribbons in my hair. She said I said "surreal" three times in one sentence and she couldn't stand me. I don't remember that, but I do remember trying very, very hard to fit in. On the senior page of my yearbook, it said, "Mary Stuart Masterson came back after 10 years, and she had to hurry back to the theater where she was starring in, writing, directing, choreographing, dancing in and producing a show called 'Mary Mary.'" I found it offensive, but it sort of indicated my role in the school—I sort of did everything.

WHEN DID YOU DECIDE YOU WANTED TO BECOME AN ACTRESS?

I've wanted to act ever since I can remember but, on one level, I didn't want to do it just because it was available to me. I couldn't stand the idea of nepotism—it made me want to puke. I tried to do everything but act; dancing was my creative outlet. I think I learned to act through learning how to choreograph, improvise and that sort of thing. Choreography taught me how to physicalize a thought, an emotion or a concept in an abstract way, yet still maintaining a specific meaning for me. If you have a specific idea or thought, you can abstract it and make it a physical movement that speaks to the heart without having to speak to the mind.

WAS THERE ANYTHING THAT PROPELLED YOU TO DECIDE TO BECOME AN ACTRESS?

Yes, getting a part in a movie, but I really didn't consider myself an actress until after doing "Lily Dale." I reveled in rehearsal and preparation for that play. I always used to prepare, but I never really enjoyed the process and allowed myself the freedom to really just go for it. It was the first time I felt I made decisions of my own volition. You really learn to commit onstage; on film, there's always something that kind of holds you back a little bit. I really believe in rehearsal now, especially for film. You can't be truly spontaneous until you have the whole structure and arc of a character worked out in your mind; you have to know what you're trying to do in every scene and in every moment. If you have all that down and you know your lines, you're totally free to do anything you want within the boundaries of choice. That's a joy. Once you learn to walk and chew gum at the same time, you can jump rope at the same time, too.

HOW DO YOU FEEL ABOUT MOST OF THE SCRIPTS YOU'RE SUBMITTED?

The biggest problem in scriptland is that no one has a decent story. Studios are into doing "concepts"—they'll say, "Let's do a movie about a girl who's in the rodeo." That's OK, but what *happens*? In the first scene, she's riding in the rodeo, in the

next scene she's riding in the rodeo, and so on. Nothing happens, nothing changes, she doesn't learn anything and the audience is not enlightened. What happened to the story?

WHAT DO YOU LOOK FOR IN A SCRIPT?

I look for a good story and characters that aren't in any way stereotypical. I don't think anyone in the world is truly stereotypical—there's always something different going on with them. I look for being able to see under the surface. I look for quirky characters that try, struggle and overcome obstacles.

WHAT KIND OF ROLES ARE YOU LOOKING FOR?

I want to play people who have problems that concern me, too. I'd love to play people from very different lifestyles than me. I want to play white trash, a journalist, a paralegal and women with brains. No one thinks a woman under 30 can have brains anymore.

HOW DO YOU APPROACH A ROLE AND WHAT KIND OF PREPARATION DO YOU DO?

First I'll read the script three times to get an overview. I try to remember my first instincts when I read it so I don't overthink it. Then I go through a process of over-complicating and simplifying the character by asking myself questions and doing all sorts of research; I get absorbed in the research so I can come up with some original ideas. I feel like that's my ammunition—that gives me confidence. Then I usually do sensory exercises as they relate to my character. That involves an hour and a half of relaxation work and then going back to specific events of my past to get sensory elements that are relevant to my character. Then I learn all my lines and talk to the director at length to find out what his vision is so we can have a common vision, or at least know what the other person is attempting to do. Misunderstanding can happen real easy.

WHEN YOU TAKE A PART, DO YOU CONSIDER WHAT EFFECT THAT ROLE AND FILM WILL HAVE ON PEOPLE?

Yes, but at the same time, I don't think it's my place to preach to people. I think my role is to truthfully play a part, no matter how ugly or sinister it may be. As long as it's truthfully played and not exploitive, then I hope people can make up their own minds. My job is to try to empower them. America is the most apathetic country in the world right now—I think television does that. My choice is not to do movies with stereotypes, that have 500 murders per hour or that make Russia look like the bad guy. I went to Russia with a group of actors organized by SANE/FREEZE; the project was called Filmmakers Exchange. We made a documentary to bring back for high school students around the country. We put together footage from our trip with fifties red-scare propaganda and clips from *Red Dawn* and films like that.

WHAT WAS GOING TO RUSSIA LIKE?

I was so excited to go, but the moment I left, I felt kind of panicked. I was scared, but I didn't want to feel that way. The whole point of the trip for me was to do away with cold-war stereotypes. When I got there, I was moved to see that people in the Soviet Union want peace even more than we do.

WHAT OTHER SOCIAL ISSUES ARE IMPORTANT TO YOU?

I'm for a nuclear freeze and I'm really concerned about the environment. I recycle my newspapers and return my bottles, but I'm trying to find out how I can conserve water and energy and help control pollution. It's such a huge problem right now—all of our natural resources are dwindling and people don't even notice. It's lemming sort of behavior. If we don't kill each other with a bomb, then how are we going to survive on this planet anyway?

WHAT ARE YOU DOING TO MAKE A DIFFERENCE?

I did the Russia documentary. Sarah Parker, some other actors and myself are working for the Committee for Peace in Central America, trying to help them raise money. Jane Fonda and Tom Hayden have been helping young actors and actresses

like me by taking them under their wings, and they've been extremely generous with their time and information. I've been checking a lot of things out.

WHAT'S THE BIGGEST MISCONCEPTION ABOUT YOU?

Probably that I take myself extremely seriously. I think everyone thinks I'm incredibly serious and that I have no sense of humor, and that's not true. I'm serious, but I'm no math teacher. Math teachers are the most boring people in the world.

It's weird, people think they know you. From a fan that's a compliment, because that means you've achieved something. From people in the business, it really pisses me off because they'll say, "She's this and she's that," and, "I know Mary Stuart Masterson and this is her." People think they can predict you and package you into a McDonald's clamshell thing, and it's not true. Hollywood tries so hard to work by formula, but it never works.

WHAT HAS BEEN YOUR BIGGEST SACRIFICE FOR SUCCESS?

I feel I've sacrificed my education, which I really value on one hand, but on the other hand I'm glad I quit college when I did—it would have made me so in my head, so analytical and so cerebral. Then I wouldn't be able to work so much off of instinct, impulse and emotions—I would be too analytical.

IF YOU COULD PLAY SOMEONE IN AN ONSCREEN BIOGRAPHY, WHO WOULD IT BE AND WHY?

Louise Brooks. I'm fascinated with her because she was a woman with so much power over people, yet you could never tell if she was being manipulated or if she was the one doing the manipulating. It's that power of attraction and repulsion that intrigues me. She's innocent yet tainted.

WHAT SPIRITUAL THINGS ARE IMPORTANT TO YOU?

Staying true to myself and accepting the fact that there was something happening before the Big Bang. Whether you call it God, Buddha, Allah, or you don't call it, there's a force inside and it has to do with nature. There's something watching over us that we're also a part of and that we have to be respectful of.

WHAT'S YOUR BIGGEST FEAR?

Nuclear holocaust.

DO YOU THINK THERE'S A SHORTAGE OF GOOD WOMEN'S ROLES IN HOLLYWOOD TODAY?

There's always been a lot of bad parts for women, and a lot of bad parts for men. Now, I think, relative to the sixties or seventies, parts are outrageously *good* for women. What you really have to do is develop roles yourself; otherwise you end up playing sweet-and-boring or ballbusting executive. People don't fit into categories like that.

WHY ARE THERE NO LEADING LADIES IN HOLLYWOOD LIKE THERE WERE DURING THE STUDIO SYSTEM ERA?

It drives me nuts. The big actresses of today—Meryl Streep, Jessica Lange, Sally Field, Glenn Close and people like that—have all done it for themselves: found books to adapt, found scripts and so on. What I find happening, though, is that they are playing women in men's roles—always a woman doing something a man can do instead of just being a woman. That's why I'm so fascinated by Louise Brooks—she had interesting women's problems.

IF TWO OTHER ACTRESSES WERE UP FOR THE SAME ROLE AS YOU, ALL THREE OF YOU WERE EQUAL IN TERMS OF LOOKS, TALENT, ETC., WHY SHOULD A DIRECTOR CHOOSE YOU OVER THE OTHER TWO ACTRESSES FOR THE PART?

I'm willing to try new things and I don't make ordinary choices.

HOW DO YOU FEEL YOU FIT INTO THE CONTEXT OF THE NEW BREED?

The interesting thing about the new breed is that we don't all work together, we come from different places and we don't all know each other. You can't put us all in one category. There's no hook—we're individuals.

Aidan Quinn

On his return to America after living in Dublin, Ireland, for six months when he was 19, Aidan Quinn worked as a roofer. One morning he was sitting on the 28th floor of a building that overlooked Lake Michigan, watching some of his co-workers getting drunk and stoned, when he realized he wanted more out of life than he was getting; it was then he decided to become an actor.

Aidan had seen a lot of plays in Dublin, and that experience had sparked his initial interest in acting. He saw film and theater not just as an opportunity to get more out of life, but as a way to *give* more.

Aidan's first film role was in *Reckless*. He was cast as a Deanesque smalltown rebel, with Daryl Hannah as his love interest. While the film did just moderately well it propelled Aidan into the category of a romantic leading man; it was a role he chose to reject.

Instead, for his next two projects, Aidan chose Susan Seidelman's offbeat comedy *Desperately Seeking Susan* and the acclaimed NBC special, *An Early Frost*. Today, Aidan's choices are morally based; he only selects roles in which he sees merit. He has chosen the true path of an actor.

WHAT IS YOUR BIGGEST FEAR?

My biggest fear is being swayed by ego and crap and not finding my true path.

DO YOU FEEL YOU'RE ON YOUR TRUE PATH?

In the past few years, I've run into a lot of conflicts about being in this business. There's one side of me that's seriously thought about quitting. I realize now, though, that I'm kidding myself. Maybe one day I'll quit, but that day is nowhere near—I have work to do and things to accomplish. This is the only work I know how to do; I'm not particularly skilled in anything else. There are things I'd like to say and money I'd like to make from this business. I want to work. As difficult as it's been, this business has been good to me.

WHAT DO YOU LIKE BEST ABOUT SUCCESS?

It's a double-edged sword. On one hand, I feel good about being validated, and on the other hand, I question who and where it comes from. It makes my responsibility and duty to my craft and to my vision and path in life that much more important. I like having the money, the freedom and the ability to do things with money that otherwise I wouldn't be able to do.

DO YOUR FANS EVER PUT PRESSURE ON YOU?

It hasn't been that much of a hassle. There have been times when some girl gets my number somehow and will keep calling, or they will show up—and it's annoying for my wife and myself. But most of the fans I meet are sweet and considerate. I'm not really *famous* famous, though; if I was, that might be really scary. But then again, I believe you create your own reality, and I won't create a reality I can't handle. If I do, it's probably my fault, or at least a good part of it is my fault. You have to only create things in your life you can handle. I could have easily become very famous

years ago, and I didn't want to. If I was just into that, I would have taken certain scripts that I turned down, but I knew I wouldn't have been able to handle it.

IF TWO OTHER ACTORS WERE UP FOR THE SAME ROLE AS YOU, AND ALL THREE OF YOU WERE EQUAL IN TERMS OF LOOKS, TALENT, ETC., WHY SHOULD A DIRECTOR CHOOSE YOU OVER THE OTHER TWO?

Everyone's spirit is special. I've never been in a situation where two other actors were up for the same role where I thought they could do the role better than me. I don't mean I could score 100 points and they could only score 99, but I think my spirit could do something special. To me, when you're doing good acting, it's not *you* doing it—the best acting I've ever done was not done by me. When you do your homework, have a good director, have a good script and work with other good actors—and that combination is a rarity—and you do some prayers or the voice of the character you're playing needs to be heard, something other than yourself takes over. Those rare moments are the best moments in acting. I think he should pick me because I start with a sense of honesty.

WHAT ARE YOU PASSIONATE ABOUT?

I'm passionate about battling the bad, the dark side of life with the good, the light. I'm passionate about the truth.

WHAT WAS YOUR CHILDHOOD LIKE?

I grew up in Rockford and Chicago, Illinois, and in Ireland. Both of my parents are Irish. I grew up with the feeling of being an outsider, and I never understood why. When we lived in Rockford, they treated me differently because my parents had accents. It was an area where there

were very few immigrants; most people there were from families whose ancestors had lived in America for generations. They would call us foreigners, and my feeling of alienation was strengthened by my parents' referring to Americans as "them" and to us as something different.

DID YOU FEEL LIKE LESS OF AN OUTSIDER WHEN YOU LIVED IN IRELAND?

I went to school in Ireland when I was four and when I was 13 and 14. In the beginning it was the same thing over there. To the Irish kids, I was a Yank. What I had to do very quickly was adapt—I also wanted to. My accent changed so much in two months, when I started school, most kids did not know I was American. They thought I was from Burr, where I had spent the summer, and they gave me shit for being from the country. When they found out I was American, they were really confused. It took time to be accepted, but I had more friends in two months there than I ever did in Rockford.

WHAT WAS YOUR FIRST ROLE AS AN ACTOR?

I played a young poet who goes from the Midwest to New York City. He meets up with a Delmore Schwartz sort of character and he befriends and idolizes this guy. The play is called "The Man In 605," and it takes place in a rundown motel in New York City, where my character works as a bellhop.

WHAT WERE YOUR GOALS WHEN YOU FIRST STARTED OUT AND HOW HAVE THEY CHANGED?

I don't have any goals; I don't know what the word means. I have aspirations. When I hear the word "goals," I think of something that sets someone off—that blinds them to a pinpoint rather than focusing on something that's real. My vision of what I want to do with acting is more open than that. I don't know exactly what it is, except that I would like to save the world—nothing less. I'd like to do that by being able to portray roles—be they good guys or selfish pricks—that make the audience more aware of themselves and each other.

HOW DO YOU FEEL ABOUT THE MAJORITY OF SCRIPTS YOU'RE SUBMITTED?

The majority of scripts I get are good for lighting wood stoves, fireplaces and for recycling to put the paper to better purposes.

WHAT DO YOU LOOK FOR IN A SCRIPT?

Ideally, I look for something that's a challenge. For instance, I recently played Stanley Kowalski in "A Streetcar Named Desire" on Broadway. That's about as diametrically opposite to me as I can possibly imagine, and it's a wonderful role by a great writer who was saying something about people.

WHAT KIND OF ROLES ARE YOU LOOKING FOR?

I'd like to do something funny, but what I want to do and what I *will* do are two different things. What you want to play is what you sort of formulate as an ideal. I like great roles like Marc Antony, Romeo and Hamlet; I've played Hamlet and I will eventually play the others. I believe you create your own reality, but it's never as easy as it sounds. It's always through a labyrinth of side turns, backups, sidetracks—and then something you want happens.

DO YOU DO ANYTHING CON-

SCIOUSLY TO CREATE YOUR OWN REALITY?

Yeah. I think it comes down to faith, belief and doing the dirt time of the discipline in order to create something to come true. The problem with this business on those lines is that getting certain roles often doesn't have anything to do with your talent or whether or not you're right for a role—it's more politically motivated. It's—and let me preface this by saying I loathe this word—*hot* or not. It's such a loathsome word because it implies coldness as well.

HOW DO YOU APPROACH A ROLE AND WHAT KIND OF PREPARATION DO YOU DO?

There's a lot of simple homework I do. I will write down every word that every other character says about my character. I note who says what and when they say it. I create a background, a paste, but not too specific because I don't want to close the book on it; I don't want to live in a closed structure, especially in rehearsal. Right now I'm trying to gain weight for a role because I'm too skinny. I read and watch movies of the time period of a project and try to find out what was going on in the day-to-day world then. I use my imagination.

DO YOU CONSIDER WHAT EFFECT A FILM WILL HAVE ON PEOPLE BEFORE TAKING A ROLE?

I must see some good in the film, and ideally I'd like to think it will have a good effect, but I'm not so indulgent as to think everything I do is going to have an effect, period. It's a little arrogant for me to try to predict the end role of something in the process. There are many possibilities. I certainly thought *Early Frost* could potentially have an effect on the way the world views people with AIDS or homosexuals, and other roles could affect this or that—but I'm too involved in the work to really think about that.

IS STUDYING IMPORTANT TO YOUR GROWTH AS AN ACTOR?

I study every day, but I don't study *acting*. I read books about it, and I take things from the books I read. Uta Hagen's book is wonderful in getting actors to get very specific, which is important. There's nothing worse than vague generalities. The best studying for me, though, is doing.

WHAT IS THE DIFFERENCE IN THE ACTING PROCESS FOR YOU IN DOING THEATER AS OPPOSED TO FILM?

Theater is much more satisfying for me. It's much more embodying, because you're using your entire body. You have the attention of the audience and their energy; it's up to you, the director and the other actors to do something with the raw materials you have. There's something primal, tribal and almost religious about good theater, but there's nothing worse than *bad* theater—it makes me feel like a dried-up prune. With film, the actual doing of it doesn't enable you to achieve immediate emotional satisfaction like that, because it's so broken up. You can possibly feel like that sitting in the audience at the end with the music and if everything works. It's very difficult to feel any continuity, and I can never forget there are 40 people standing in front of my face; whereas, in theater, because of the lights, you can't really see the audience—you know they're there, but you're not looking at them. On the last film I did, I experimented by admitting the crew was there instead of trying to block them out—I

tried to *use* it instead of withdrawing into an artificial square box. Film is very delicate and frustrating to me, yet very exciting with what you can do with it. Its potential is amazing.

IS BEING AN ACTOR A STRUGGLE FOR YOU?

It's always a struggle; I always want to quit. I've never worked on a role where I didn't come to a point where I said, "This is so bad, and I'm so terrible in it—acting is silly." I have to get past that point by using that. It helps me, because that's how I feel in *life* a lot. There are times when I feel everything in my life is so absurd and I just want to throw up my arms and laugh. So I *do*, and then I move on.

WHAT HAS BEEN YOUR BIGGEST SACRIFICE FOR SUCCESS?

My biggest sacrifice for success as an actor is not being able to pursue spiritual things full-time.

WHAT SPIRITUAL THINGS ARE IMPORTANT TO YOU?

It's plain and simple—enlightenment. But I don't think that happens until you take your last walk, because, if it did, you would probably *take* your last walk. I don't believe you wake up on top of a mountain after six months and say, "Now I know everything; now I am enlightened." I think holy men who lead that life should get off the top of the mountain, go back into the towns and cities, teach, talk and spread the word. They shouldn't be so fucking selfish, living alone in bliss on top of a mountain. That's easy in a way. At first it might be difficult, because we are conditioned to live differently—but if you were brought up in the wilderness, living that way is pretty blissful, pretty simple. If you

are in tune with nature and Mother Earth, deer will actually show up and offer themselves to you—it's not that difficult. What *is* difficult is to realize what's happening to the planet, and to take it upon yourself to do something about it. Not you *should* do something, but you *will* do something. I believe the earth is dying and there's not a lot of time to turn it around—but it is possible.

SO WHAT ARE YOU DOING TO MAKE A DIFFERENCE?

I'm trying not to pollute and be more conscious. My wife and I do recycling. Right now, I'm living in a house in the foothills of a mountain. It's not difficult to feel reverence for the earth, the trees, the mountains, the sky and the snow.

IF YOU COULD DO AN ON SCREEN BIOGRAPHY OF SOMEONE, WHO WOULD IT BE AND WHY?

There's a guy named Grey Owl I'd like to play. He was an Englishman who came over to Canada in the late 1800s and hung out with this Indian tribe, and then traveled the world and passed himself off as a native Indian. He became quite well-known and famous, and he wrote about his life as "Grey Owl, the Indian." It turned out to be a fallacy. What he did was invent his own path from living with these Indians for a while, because it was the most romantic way of living to him.

WHAT IS THE BIGGEST MISCONCEPTION ABOUT YOU?

That I'm difficult to work with—because I'm really not. I am if I'm dealing with low-life amateurs or money-grubbing producers who know nothing about the script they're producing, but not with directors or other actors. I'm a perfectionist, but what other way is there to be?

Keanu Reeves

Keanu Reeves could care less about becoming a "movie star." Success, he feels, is all relative anyway, and for Keanu, pure passion and true happiness are derived from one thing—acting.

For the past few years, Keanu has been starring in one film after another, yet little has materially changed in his life. He still lives with a roommate in the same small, dark, sparsely furnished apartment in a rent-controlled section of Los Angeles. He still only bathes once or twice a week. There is still a slightly gamey smell emanating from his bedroom, where mountains of unlaundered clothes cover the floor. He still wails to the Butthole Surfers, and he still drinks cheap red wine for recreation during his little time off.

Keanu seems oblivious to his surroundings. He says he keeps thinking about getting a new place, but he just never gets around to it. Besides, it's not *that* bad; it's home and fine for now. He has plenty of room to set up his amps and all of his bass equipment, and he has his own bedroom. What's much more important to him at this point is getting quality roles and growing as an actor.

Since enrolling in a night-school drama class in Toronto, Ontario, when he was 17, "just because it seemed like the thing to do," Keanu has been obsessed with acting. The class provided him with the tools to create a new perspective, self-respect and something to live for. At the time, Keanu was attending his fourth high school in five years, living aimlessly with no real goals, resigned to the notion that he might be making pasta for the rest of his life.

An existence devoid of material things didn't really bother him, though; he says he could still live without a lot of worldly goods—as long as he could go on acting forever.

WHY DID YOU GO TO SO MANY HIGH SCHOOLS?

They all seemed to make sense. When I got out of grade eight, I picked the best academic school, even though I wasn't a very good student. I was the only one from my school who went there, so that was sort of weird—oh, the agony and ecstasy that was grade nine. One day I was playing basketball in grade ten and a friend of mine asked me if I wanted to go audition for the performing arts high school. I did, and I got in. I was happy for a while, but then I got kicked out.

WHY?

Because I was greasy and running around a lot. I was just a little too rambunctious and shot my mouth off once too often. I

was not generally the most well-oiled machine in the school. I was just getting in their way, I guess.

WHEN DID YOU DECIDE TO BECOME AN ACTOR?

That didn't really happen until I was 17 or 18. I started taking acting courses at night. It just seemed the thing to do. Most of it was out of respect for acting. I worked at some Stanislavsky stuff and I was playing around with sense memory. I started crashing auditions and then I got some jobs and joined the community theater. Then I got an agent.

WHAT WAS YOUR VERY FIRST ROLE?

I was in summer camp and I was in the

chorus of "Damn Yankees." I think I was nine. That was my first dramatic appearance.

WHAT WAS YOUR FIRST PROFESSIONAL ROLE?

Hanging In, CBC, Toronto. It is a local television show about some counseling place in the inner city. It's a Godsend for young actors in Toronto—it's still going. They give lots of roles out to young kids. It was a three-camera shoot, and I played a tough street kid. I wore stupid clothes and had no idea of what I was doing. My line was, "Hey lady, can I use the shower?" After that, I did more community theater and a Coke commercial.

Then I did a play in Toronto called "Wolf Boy." I played a guy named Bernie, a suicidal jock who goes into an insane asylum—a place where they put people who are emotionally disturbed. There's this guy in the next room who thinks he is a wolf. He fucks with me and eventually we fall in love. He kills me because I'm a bonehead and I ultimately can't love him. In the last scene of the play, he stabs me; the lights go down, and it cuts to another scene with him, my father and a nurse. I'm lying on the stage, tons of blood all over me, and he's hunched over me in this white light, slurping blood off of my chest, licking my mouth. The poster depicted us in white T-shirts with our hair slicked back, all wet, and he's almost kissing me while kind of grinning. So the first couple of shows, all these leather boys came; that was funny . . . but it was also scary, because the first week I was really bad. I got better, though, and by the end of it, I was pretty rad, thrashing-cool.

WHY DID YOU MOVE TO L.A.?

Two years ago I was at a point where I had done the most I could do in Toronto. I was tired of playing the best friend, thug number one and the tall guy. I read for a Disney Movie of the Week called *Young Again*. No one liked me but the director. He hooked me up with Hildy Gottlieb at ICM. I flew out to meet her and eventually got my green card. I got into my dumpy 1969 Volvo and drove here with $3,000. I stayed at my stepfather's and proceeded to go into the darkness—the darkness that is L.A.

SO YOU DID *RIVER'S EDGE*; THEN WHAT?

I did a film called *The Night Before*. It seems in Hollywood you have to do a kooky comedy to lose your cinematic Hollywood virginity. It's a coming-of-age movie—you know, guy wants girl, guy gets girl. It was the first time I became involved in the process of making a film, since I was in every scene. Then I did a film called *Bill and Ted's Excellent Adventure*, directed by Steven Harrick. I got to play a child of nature, someone who is almost an idiot savant—except he's not that smart, but he's pure and good. He's got a good soul; he doesn't judge anyone. Then I did a film called *Permanent Record* for Paramount about suicide. Paramount took some risks. Fred Allen shot it. It looks so amazing. Alan Boyce plays a boy named David who's a songwriter who commits suicide, and I play his best friend.

WHAT WERE YOUR GOALS WHEN YOU FIRST STARTED OUT AND HOW HAVE THEY CHANGED NOW?

I jumped into acting without an ultimate goal, and it's just recently that I've realized that if I don't have any goals, people are going to fuck with me—I really hate that. In the immediacy of being in Hollywood, now in my life as it is, I would like to play a very neurotic, crazy, preferably mean, evil character—I would like to play someone who's just fucking *ugly*. Most of the characters I've played so far have been good people; they all, in a sense, are in possession of sort of a naivete. I guess that's me, and I'd like to explore and exploit some other stuff.

HOW DO YOU FEEL ABOUT MOST SCRIPTS YOU ARE SUBMITTED?

Most of them are bad.

WHAT DO YOU LOOK FOR IN A SCRIPT?

I want to be enlightened, dude. I don't know, just interesting stories, interesting people, character development, ideas being posed, clash/conflicts, hate, love, war, death, success, fame, failure, redemption, salvation, death, hell, sin, good food, bad food, nice smells, colors and big tits.

HOW DO YOU PREPARE FOR A ROLE?

All I can say is that I try to give and I try to learn.

WOULD YOU DO A NUDE SCENE?

Only if it was a good nude scene; I won't do superfluous nudity. If you are asking me if I am embarrassed about my body—sometimes.

DO YOU STILL STUDY ACTING?

Yeah. Studying has a definite place in my world. I'm 23 and I've been studying since I was 17—16 if you count the performing arts high school. My studying has been very nomadic and has been a fairly wide range of approaches. Studying is important; there's still a lot I don't know.

WAS FINDING THE RIGHT MANAGER OR AGENT HARD FOR YOU?

No. They sort of all serendipitously came together. I thank the gods. You know, one thing that's cool about Hollywood is that if you somehow happen to be an actor in a film that makes a lot of money, you get power. By power I don't mean too much power, like Eddie Murphy—being so far out there that you're no longer accessible as an actor. But I would like to have enough interest in me so that I can make a difference.

WHAT HAS BEEN YOUR BIGGEST SACRIFICE FOR SUCCESS?

Love. . . .

WHAT IS THE BIGGEST MISCONCEPTION ABOUT YOU?

That I'm clean.

WHAT DO YOU LIKE MOST ABOUT BEING AN ACTOR?

I almost said chicks and sex and fucking and money—but that hasn't happened yet. What do I like most about being an actor? Acting! The best thing for me about being an actor is acting. I mean, what else is there?

DOES DEALING WITH YOUR FANS EVER PUT ANY PRESSURE ON YOU?

Yes. Very bizarre—sometimes it's fun. Most of the fan mail I get makes me cry, though. Occasionally I get letters that are so amazingly beautiful and sincere, and I know that I've moved someone and that makes me feel fucking amazing. I totally write them back and go, "Here man, thank you. *Thank* you." Other times, I just don't deal with it at all.

DO YOU EVER GET RECOGNIZED?

It's happened about 12 times. I feel like a young pubic hair—you know, I keep getting checked out and played with sometimes. The heaviest thing that happened to me was when I met this kid, about 17, who looked like Matt, my character in *River's Edge*, and he said, "Man, you're my idol," and he gave me all this free food in this restaurant he worked in. That was really cool.

IF YOU COULD STAR IN AN ONSCREEN BIOGRAPHY OF ANYONE, WHO WOULD IT BE AND WHY?

The young part of me would love to play Rimbaud. Imagine writing those fucking sonnets in Latin at 17 and telling teachers they're full of shit. And then, at 19, 20, being totally disillusioned, and for the next 20 years, leading a life of debauchery, and, ultimately, dying in the gutter. That sort of appeals to my self-destructive, artistic, cool kind of deep side.

WHAT SPIRITUAL THINGS ARE IMPORTANT TO YOU?

I'm going to get more wine. Oh yeah, man, if we're talking about spirituality, man, I'm going to be like drinking wine. "I'll be going in the gutter" is the man's essence—and the man's essence is in the gutter, man. . . . Spiritual? Well, um, I don't involve myself in any organized religion. I checked that out when I was 11; since then I haven't needed it.

DO YOU BELIEVE IN GOD?

Here we go. God? OK, sure. I seem to pay some petty respect whenever I talk about my success. I talk about my fear of retribution for my success—that I must pay for it. I guess in some sort of deep-rooted way, I feel I haven't. I guess I'm paying tribute to irony. Irony can make you bitter, but, yeah, I guess I believe in God. No, I don't believe in God. I don't know. These things are still in turmoil.

WHAT IS YOUR BIGGEST FEAR?

If I knew that [he sips his wine] Um, . . . That my underwear would have a shit stain on it if I'm ever with a woman that I've never slept with before. That's a major fear—that would be a drag. God, it's like everything is a flash. All I can say is that I'm 23 and there's some poem—I don't know who wrote it, probably Walt Whitman in his youth—dealing with young men and their fears.

DO YOU MANAGE YOUR MONEY WELL?

No! But better than I used to. I used to live my life out of a basket. I had this killer Kellogs commercial once, made tons of money, and I cashed the check and put all the cash in a basket. I'd get a residual check, and I'd go to the bank and say, "I'd like to cash this check for $4,000," and they'd ask me if I wanted to open up an account with them. I'd say, "No, just give me my money," and for the next year I'd say, "well, I've got money," and I'd live my life out of the basket. Then things got more complicated. When things get complicated, I bail. Now I've hired accountants and I pay *careful* attention . . . kind of. I'm still sort of delinquent about that. I've learned from acting that simple things grow strong. Yeah, I'm trying to keep my life simple. I'm basically a pretty rudimentary fellow: "Think of Ben Hur when you write my name; think biblical.—*Keanu Reeves*."

WHO WOULD BE THE IDEAL WOMAN YOU COULD BE CAST OPPOSITE?

Oh, I don't know, man. Who would I like to fuck the most? Meryl Streep.

WHY?

Because even if I wasn't good, she could fake it the best.

HAVE YOU SLEPT WITH MOST OF YOUR LEADING LADIES?

Not at all, man. I'm practically a celibate monk—it's true. I would actually most like to act with Eleanora Duse, who was a contemporary of Sarah Bernhardt. Those were two amazing women, and they represented a real dichotomy in acting styles. Sarah was very theatrical, melodramatic; Eleanora was more straight. She revolutionized a more natural acting style.

IF TWO OTHER ACTORS WERE UP FOR THE SAME PART AS YOU, AND ALL THREE OF YOU WERE EQUAL IN TERMS OF LOOKS, TALENT, EXPERIENCE, ETC., WHY SHOULD THE DIRECTOR PICK YOU?

I don't know—that's hard.

HOW DO YOU FEEL YOU FIT INTO THE CONTEXT OF *THE NEW BREED*?

Ha! OK, this is what I feel is happening with actors in Hollywood. A lot of people I've been working with have a sense of darkness and seriousness about their point of view of acting. I think there are a lot of heavy actors who are going to come out and surprise people. They are going to help Hollywood. They are very sincere and generally well-read and smart about what they are doing. They have a strong point of view about their acting and their place in the world. We are getting more theatrical in our acting styles. Film in that sense is taking more risks. Even the actors who aren't doing anything yet but being cute and themselves will hopefully in the future push and expand their limits. We *hope*—because I'd like to spend six bucks and feel it was worth it.

The New Breed for me has some sort of connotation and reflection about the past—the brat pack/the method/the studios/the Russians/the English/the Americans/the truth. People are bored with being so literal. We need some more of that good old thirties, forties and fifties surrealism again, especially in our comedy. Audiences are ready to see more intelligent work.

When I go to see *Beverly Hills Cop 2* in Times Square at midnight, and people are getting stoned and talking to the screen, I don't think they are satisfied. I realized being a semi-successful actor in Hollywood brings certain responsibilities with it. Some of them I enjoy, but some of them are sort of weird. I guess I'm in the new breed because I'm 23, and I'm not 46 or 52. I'm not Dennis Hopper; I'm just doing what I'm doing—trying, at least. I'm trying to pursue what I'm curious about, trying to survive, and hopefully not be fucked up the ass by irony and the gods.

WHAT DO YOU REMEMBER MOST ABOUT PLAYING IN THE BACKYARD OF THE HOUSE YOU GREW UP IN?

The sound or cars racing by. Whoosh. Whoosh. More cars racing by. The garden. The wind blows through it. Wishing the wind would pick me up and carry me away. Wanting to be somewhere else. My treehouse. It's an old apple tree, sort of like an old man with one arm missing. It just leans out and reaches up into the sky. The elbow is connected with a string hanging down and a plastic tire that was bought at Sears. I swing on it, but I never really like it because it isn't a real tire. From my treehouse I can see everything; it is my control tower. I play with my GI Joes. If they fall off, they die. One time a GI Joe's arm falls off, and I pretend he is an amputee from the war. In the wintertime I can jump off of the elbow of the old man like a paratrooper. I can fly for a few seconds.

Once I ran away to my treehouse. It was a Sunday in the middle of February. It had just snowed, but the sun was out. I packed up everything that was important to me: my GI Joes, my stamp collection and a few clothes. Dinner was being served, but I didn't want any. The house was filled with the smell of roast beef, served every Sunday at the same time, which I hated. I had my Donny & Marie lunch box filled with cookies. I put on my jacket and marched out the door. Everyone took me very seriously. They said, "Go. Good luck." I sat in the corner of my treehouse shaking. Five minutes seemed like a lifetime. What was I going to do? I went back into the house, dejected. I had failed at a young age.

IF I WERE TO ASK ONE OF YOUR FRIENDS FROM HIGH SCHOOL WHAT YOU WERE LIKE, WHAT WOULD THEY SAY AND HOW WOULD THEY DESCRIBE YOU?

Weird—I think that sums it up, They thought I was weird because I was into juggling and riding my unicycle. I was into different things than most kids who grew up in Buckfield [Maine]. I remember when I had my hair parted down the middle when it was big, and everyone thought I was gay. When they asked me if I was gay, I said yes to piss them off, but I was never really gay. I thought it would be a great ploy to get girls because they would try to convert me. I was wrong. It backfired.

Patrick Dempsey

It is the hour in which day slips into night. As the sun silently slips into the sea, streaks of purple and pink light illuminate the sky. The waves rock gently against the shore, and as the day ends in a final burst of iridescence, there is a deep sense of peace and tranquility. Patrick Dempsey loves walking along the ocean during this magical hour.

The beach, a few blocks from his home in Santa Monica, California, is a place where Dempsey can be alone to think and center himself. Aside from acting, inner peace and enlightenment are the most important things in his life.

A student of Gurumayi (Swami Chidvilasananda, a disciple of Muktananda), Dempsey practices Siddah Yoga, often meditating for many hours at a time in a single sitting. He says his career did not take off until his "divine inner energy" or "shaktipat" was opened up by his guru.

In the two years since his spiritual awakening, Dempsey has starred in three feature films and in an episode of American Playhouse for PBS. He has also overcome a serious case of dyslexia, mastering reading and writing for the first time in his life. Despite the less than enthusiastic reviews received by his first few projects, Dempsey has been consistently singled out for his acting prowess. He attributes his success to his commitment to creating believable characters as well as the support and guidance of his coach and manager Rocky Parker.

Keeping everything in perspective, however, he feels he is just starting out and has a lot to learn. One of Dempsey's dreams is to study at the Royal Academy of Dramatic Arts in London, and to develop his skills as a classical actor. Fame and fortune are the antithesis of his priorities. All Patrick Dempsey wants is mainstream acceptance while maintaining his integrity.

HOW DID YOU GET INTO RIDING A UNICYCLE AND JUGGLING?

I wanted to be a ski racer; I was a State of Maine champion. I saw Ingmar Stenmark in the 1984 Olympics, and he was riding a unicycle, and I decided that's what I needed to do to improve my skiing. Through the unicycle, a shop teacher named Paul McKinney introduced me to juggling and one thing led to another.

HOW DID LEARNING TO JUGGLE LEAD TO A CAREER AS A FEATURE FILM STAR?

I entered a competition called Talent America. I had a three-minute juggling/comedy routine. I won the Maine preliminary, and I went to New York City for the national competition, hoping to get an agent so I could start auditioning for plays. I ended up winning, and I got a huge trophy as well as an agent. A few weeks after I won, my new agent asked me if I'd fly down to New York City to audition for the San Francisco company of "Torch Song Trilogy," a Broadway play. I said sure, but I had no idea of how I'd afford to get down there. My dad took a loan out of the bank; I went, auditioned and got the part. I never really went back home to Maine after that. I usually say I ran away

from home because it sounds more glamorous, and I like it that way—but the truth was, I had the opportunity to do "Torch Song Trilogy," and saw it as my ticket out of Maine.

WHY DIDN'T YOU LIKE IT IN MAINE?

I just felt it was too confining. Nobody had wild, crazy ideas; they didn't have any vision. You'd go to college and get married. It wasn't something I wanted to get into.

DID YOU FEEL LIKE YOU DIDN'T FIT IN?

I didn't really fit in, but then again, I didn't work too hard at *trying* to fit in—it just wasn't rewarding enough. I made an attempt early on, but I wanted to do my own thing, and doing my own thing in Buckfield, Maine, meant not fitting in.

WHAT WAS DOING "TORCH SONG TRILOGY" IN SAN FRANCISCO LIKE?

I was a Maine hick at the time—I still am to a certain extent—but I was really naive then. I was 17, but I looked 12, doing a gay-themed play in San Francisco. Homosexuality was freaking me out; it was new

to me and I didn't know how to react. The people in the company were really warm, so I started to relax. I didn't experiment at all because I had just lost my virginity in Maine, and that was a big thing to me. I was looking at girls. I'm more aware of what the whole experience was all about now then I was back then. I was open to it all, and I couldn't tell who was gay and who wasn't, but it didn't matter. What difference does it make, anyway?

WAS YOUR PART IN "TORCH SONG TRILOGY" YOUR FIRST ROLE AS AN ACTOR?

No. I did a play called "On Golden Pond" in the Maine Acting Company, but it was the first professional thing I'd ever done. I didn't know a thing about acting.

WHAT WERE YOUR GOALS WHEN YOU FIRST STARTED OUT?

As first my goals were to get as many girls as possible, drive the biggest car I could buy and become a big movie star. That lasted about a year. Living like that was taking me further and further away from acting, and I didn't even realize it at the time. It wasn't until I met my acting coach, Rocky, that I began to get a real understanding of acting. Everyone in America is led to believe, through interviews with "stars," that having big cars and living the fast life is what being an actor is all about. Now that I've been through all of that, I know that's not what it's all about.

DID YOU WORK DURING THIS TIME?

I worked because I got by on my cuteness, but I got terrible roles. I did this horrible movie called *Meatballs 3*—it was awful. I was ordering Dom Perignon thinking I was the coolest, hippest guy—and I was a real asshole because I didn't know about feelings, I didn't know who *I* was and I really didn't know what was going on.

WHERE WERE YOU LIVING THEN?

I was sleeping on the floor of my friend's apartment in New York City. I was irresponsible, running away from all of my problems and not dealing with anything. I was broke and getting further and further into the hole. I started hanging out with the wrong people; with the drug crowd which I didn't need.

WHAT ATTRACTED YOU TO THAT SCENE?

I was hungry for someone to hang out with. I was a new kid from Maine, getting caught up in all of this stuff. I was lucky it was six months or a year instead of six years. I had to go through that, though, to respect what I have today.

WHAT ARE YOUR GOALS AS AN ACTOR AND AS A PERSON?

It's not about making money anymore. I like money—who doesn't?—but my goal is to just do the work and to try not to get caught up in the Hollywood element. I think you can live in Hollywood and not get caught up in the bullshit. How can I put it into words? I want to do good work and find out who I am as a person. Each time out, I want to create an entirely new character. I want to be around for the next 50 years.

HOW DO YOU FEEL ABOUT THE MAJORITY OF SCRIPTS YOU ARE SUBMITTED?

I think the majority are out to make money. There are some good ones out there, but it's just beginning to turn around to meet the needs of teenagers. There are always going to be teen-exploitation movies because they make money. They're mindless movies, but sometimes, in the world we live in, we need to see things like that, so there is a need being fulfilled. I don't want to be part of that film genre anymore. I want to do films that have some kind of meaning, that touch me when I do them and touch the audience when they see them.

WHAT KINDS OF ROLES ARE YOU LOOKING FOR?

I'm looking for roles where the character has a struggle close to my struggle at the time. I believe every time I'm given a script, it's what I need to work through at that particular time. The lucky thing about being an actor is that you can work through all of your emotional troubles if you really want to commit to doing that; I need to commit even more.

HOW DO YOU APPROACH A ROLE?

It's different each time. I go over the overall flow of it, what the whole point of the movie is about, from point A to point Z. Then I chop up the script from where the transition in the middle is and break it into acts. With that blueprint, I work on developing the character. I work with dreams and I go into my inner self. There is a good technical thing coming out of that—it's very Jungian. I do a little bit of the method. I'm trying to create my *own* method.

HOW DO YOU PREPARE FOR YOUR ROLE?

I prepare more in the emotional layers: What he is going through emotionally, what's going on in a particular scene, where he's coming from, etc. It's your basic actor homework. I work from the inside out.

DO YOU CONSIDER THE EFFECT A FILM WILL HAVE ON YOUR PEERS BEFORE TAKING A ROLE?

That's one element of it. I ask myself, "Does this really need to be done?" and "Is there anything in here that I've gone through?" I don't try to go at it from the ego kind of thing that it is going to affect 200,000 teenagers across America and I'm a part of it and I'm going to change the world. It's really I Ching.

WAS FINDING THE RIGHT MANAGER/AGENT HARD FOR YOU, AND DID YOU GET RIPPED OFF ALONG THE WAY?

I got hooked up with a guy who ripped me off and took me down the wrong path a little bit, but I got out of it very quickly and met the right person. I've been very fortunate. When you start coming out of the right place and you make a conscious decision to *continue* coming out of the right place, suddenly your energy brings in that kind of energy. When I changed my idea of what I wanted to do and I started working hard, the right people started coming to me. Whatever you put out comes back to you multiplied. If you put out negative energy and anger, you get more anger back. If you put out love, you get love back.

HOW DID YOU MEET ROCKY, YOUR MANAGER AND ACTING COACH?

I met her on tour in "Brighton Beach Memoirs." No one had ever taken the time to show me anything before, and suddenly this woman said, "Let me help you," and she became my coach and helped me make decisions about my career. I toured with that show for a year, and we worked together. She gave up her career as an actress to help me. I needed someone to look out for me, and thank God her family took me in. If it wasn't for Rocky and her sons and daughter, I would not be where I am today.

WHAT HAS BEEN YOUR BIGGEST SACRIFICE FOR SUCCESS?

At first it was not going out and being cool; that was the first sacrifice. For the past three years, I've stopped living to a certain extent. I've hung out at my house, and I've gone to the opposite extreme of my days in New York. I don't know if that's a sacrifice anymore, though. Now not being true to myself all of the time is my biggest sacrifice.

IS BEING AN ACTOR EVER A STRUGGLE FOR YOU?

We label ourselves as being "actors," and that gets us into trouble. You get the attitude of, "I'm an actor now—I hang out, smoke cigarettes, wear a leather jacket and talk about 'acting.'" Yes, I am an actor, but yes, I am a human being, and I have to remember that I'm a human being *first*. I don't want to be associated with the acting. That means if I do a bad movie and fail as an actor, I don't fail as a person and I'm not a bad person. I'm working hard at getting that attitude.

WHAT DO YOU LIKE BEST ABOUT SUCCESS?

You don't have to audition, and you get a

little more respect and recognition. You walk down the street and people know you. It's like I'm back in my hometown anywhere I go. It's weird, but it's warm.

IF YOU COULD PLAY ANYONE IN AN ONSCREEN BIOGRAPHY, WHO WOULD IT BE AND WHY?

Montgomery Clift. He was one of the first actors who achieved notoriety, but got so caught up in his personal struggle it destroyed him. He had deep pain; I sometimes wish *I* had that. I have pain in my life, but I don't have it as deep as he did. I tend to go to the opposite. What I don't have I want, and what I have I don't want.

WHAT SPIRITUAL THINGS ARE IMPORTANT TO YOU?

I'm starting to meditate. I'm trying to find the path that's going to work for me. I'm into Siddah Yoga and meditation and reading books on that. I'm not spiritually enlightened, but I'm trying to get there. It's hard. I have a guru, Gurumayi. She's an Indian woman from a long lineage of Siddah yogas, who are spiritually enlightened beings through training themselves and strengthening their minds. It's a philosophy [that says] God and greatness are within ourselves. They don't say no to any God; they accept all religions. You don't have to shave your head and give them all your money. It's about yourself—dealing with yourself and dealing with your own problems. The basic philosophy is simple—love yourself. *Om namah shivaya*: I respect myself. I think the consciousness today is getting around to that.

IF THERE ARE TWO OTHER ACTORS UP FOR THE SAME PART AS YOU, AND YOU ARE ALL EQUAL IN TERMS OF LOOKS, EXPERIENCE, ETC. WHY SHOULD A DIRECTOR CHOOSE YOU OVER THE OTHER TWO ACTORS?

Why shouldn't he? Everyone gets a role because there is a certain essence in them that is that character. Even though we look alike and we are the same, there's one part of us that's different, and he'll see that part.

IF YOU WERE GRANTED THREE WISHES, WHAT WOULD THEY BE?

To be enlightened; wouldn't you wish for that? My second wish would to be married to Isabella Rosellini, and my third wish would be to be at peace with myself. I could say I'd wish to be a great actor, but let's get real. What I *really* would want would be to move through this life and move onto what life is really all about.

PATRICK, WHAT TO YOU IS PASSION?

Total commitment. Love. Have to have it and have to be doing it, and nothing is there besides it. There are moments when you look up and suddenly everything connects—those moments are passion.

HOW DO YOU FEEL YOU FIT INTO THE CONTEXT OF *THE NEW BREED*?

The new breed is happening because the old breed is dying out. There's a new consciousness among young actors—they're a lot more aware of what's going on and being true to themselves. The passion to them, as it is to me, is in the work—and that's really what it's all about, isn't it?

Martha Plimpton

Walking down Columbus Avenue in New York City, everything looks the same. The restaurants may offer different cuisines, the merchandise in the clothing boutiques may vary slightly, the bars may feature different decors, yet everything blends together and there is an underlying sameness to it all.

Manhattan's Upper West Side was not always like this, however. When Martha Plimpton was growing up, there was an edge to this part of town—a spicy blend of danger, drugs and decadence, the feeling anything could and would happen. Columbus Avenue was once a melting pot of diverse cultures, ethnic groups and creative people.

When the yuppies moved in, they homogenized the neighborhood, extinguishing the passion and excitement, squeezing out the creative element that had kept this area so vibrant and alive. Columbus Avenue turned into a sea of ostentatious superficiality—all package and no content.

Martha hasn't forgotten the way it used to be, the neighborhood and her life—tough, poor and surviving day by day. While she has been working steadily as an actress since the age of eight, reaching prominence at 11 in Richard Avedon's Calvin Klein television commercials, Martha's early childhood toughened her and made her grow up quickly.

She still lives on the Upper West Side, although she's not there very much anymore. Martha spends most her time on film locations and going on auditions in Los Angeles, where she drives around in a beat-up red Mustang she bought for a couple thousand dollars.

Martha feels her childhood prepared her for anything, yet she expects nothing, still taking it day by day.

DESCRIBE THE HOUSE AND NEIGHBORHOOD YOU GREW UP IN

I mainly grew up in apartments in New York City. The first place I can remember was a brownstone on the Upper West Side, a tenement-type place. At that time, the neighborhood was kind of shoddy. Now it's a big deal, but then it was not the best neighborhood to live in. I slept on a mattress—we didn't own a bed. It was a one-bedroom apartment, and it was always sort of dark. There were only two windows in the whole place. There was always the smell of food cooking in the halls. It was a highly Puerto Rican neighborhood, Dominican and Haitian also. At that time, I was the only white kid on my block. I was also the only white kid in kindergarten at my school. I basically grew very independent those first few years of my life.

WHAT WAS YOUR FIRST ROLE AS AN ACTRESS?

The first thing I did was an Elizabeth Swados workshop. It was a film workshop of "The Runaways," which had been on Broadway. I auditioned for the hell of it, because I happened to be there at the time. Liz had worked with my mom [actress Shelly Plimpton] before, and I got the part by accident. I've been working ever since. I did two plays after that— "The Hagadah" and another one that didn't open; it was a terrible play. My first onscreen part was as a day player in *Rollover*; I played somebody's daughter. So Alan Paluka gave me my first part in a movie. From there I did an [ABC] *Afterschool Special*; I played a bully, which was interesting, because my friends in school were bullies, but I was always wimpy. I went to school and I was always terrorized by older kids.

HOW DID YOU GET THE CALVIN KLEIN COMMERCIALS?

I went to meet Cis Corman, a casting director, and she said, "I've got this thing, but you probably won't get it because you're a little young." I was 11 years old, and my attitude was, what the hell, it's an audition. I met Dick Avedon, and it took a little persuading on his part to get Calvin Klein to use me, but he did and I got it. I never met the man, but he gave me my first big break.

NOBODY COULD BELIEVE YOU WERE 11?

No one could, and the great thing about it was that there was nothing sexual about it. They were funny commercials—they didn't mean to say anything and I had a great time doing them. From there I did my first lead in a feature film, *The River Rat*. It didn't do well at the box office, but it was the most amazing movie-making experience I've ever had; I learned so much.

WHAT DID YOU LEARN?

It's hard to say exactly what I learned in words, because that's like asking someone what they learned in high school; it's a whole experience. I learned different techniques, the typical acting shit, but most importantly, I learned how to deal with people. It was the most social time in my life. It was the most people I'd ever met or was forced to be with at one time. I've grown up with adults. My mother treated me like an adult, and I knew it was the best way to act if I wanted to be acknowledged without coming off as really precocious and obnoxious. As a result, I think I had a better grip than most kids my age, at that time, on social awareness, mannerisms and things like that. On the other hand, I knew less about kids' stuff, but I don't think I missed out.

WAS IT DIFFICULT FOR YOU TO MAKE FRIENDS WITH KIDS YOUR OWN AGE?

Maybe. Most people told me, and still tell me, that their first impression of me was that I was arrogant, haughty, obnoxious and conceited. That might be because of my attitude. It's nothing I do on purpose—it's just the way I am. I don't let many people into my inner soul.

WHAT WERE YOUR GOALS AS AN ACTRESS WHEN YOU FIRST STARTED OUT AND HOW HAVE THEY CHANGED?

I didn't have any goals when I started out, and I still don't have any goals—I don't believe in them. When you set goals, you're putting on blinders, and I don't want to do that. I want to take it as it comes and concentrate on who I am.

WHAT KINDS OF ROLES ARE YOU LOOKING FOR?

I think for an actor to say what kind of role he wants is OK, but I think it's sort of jumping the gun because there are a lot of actors out there who just want to work. I consider myself lucky to be working. I don't want to work on shit; I want to work on good things. I'll be damned if you're going to see me on *Dynasty* or anything like that. I've been lucky in my career. I've made some good choices and I've been helped into some good choices. There's been a real diversity to my roles, and there's more to come.

WHAT DO YOU LOOK FOR IN A SCRIPT?

I look for a beginning, a middle and an end. I look for a plot. When I'm reading a script, I want to be interested in it. If it doesn't interest me in the first ten pages, I usually don't finish it.

HOW DO YOU APPROACH A ROLE?

I usually read the script a few times and look at the dialogue. I don't do any preparation until I meet the director and start rehearsals, because I don't want to start something that's totally off the wall. I don't want to completely develop my character, because it could totally change when I work with the director, and that would really fuck me up. Basically, I just use common sense. I concentrate and look at it from a very weakened perspective. It's very humbling: You *have* to humble yourself if you're going to play someone else. You have to lose all of your own pride and bring on the pride of someone else— create that and make it real. You can't create someone else when you're hung up in your own shit.

HAVE YOU STUDIED ACTING AT ALL?

I've studied acting in school, but I haven't studied techniques. Most of what I've learned is from my directors. I've been very lucky—I've worked with some great directors.

SO STUDYING IS NOT IMPORTANT TO YOU AS AN ACTRESS?

I hate to say that, because I never know, but at this point, right now, it's not. I think improv classes are good, because they bring out what's already inside of you—it brings out your creativity. The reason I'm leery of acting classes, honestly, is that they sometimes instill something that isn't there yet. I don't believe in that—I think it's just confusing.

DO YOU CONSIDER WHAT EFFECT A FILM WILL HAVE ON YOUR PEERS WHEN YOU ACCEPT A ROLE?

I think it's important to consider your audience, and the fact you're young and the people who watch you are young and they idolize you, in some cases. For me, that's not the case yet, but I would never do a film that I wouldn't want to spend two hours watching. I think it's a waste of time. When you do a movie and you ask for a lot of money, *you* see the money, but the audience never sees it. A film is not about the money; a film is not about the billing. A film is about what the audience gets. As far as kids seeing me do all sorts of taboo things onscreen that teenagers are not supposed to do, I believe there's not much onscreen these days that they haven't done themselves—I really believe that. Nobody watches a movie and is shocked by what a teenager is actually doing. They're shocked because they're doing it in front of 50,000 people. We Americans seem to think that teenagers are so wholesome and don't do shit like that, but they do. I don't want to encourage it, because it's not my thing, but I believe people should do as they please. My goal is to make people feel at home when they're watching me in a movie. I want them to feel as if they know me and relate to me as a real person. I hope I'm not the type of actress who can be labeled or typecast as a certain persona; I don't want that. I don't think people should be labeled, and I don't think kids should see that example.

IS BEING AN ACTRESS EVER A STRUGGLE FOR YOU?

I think what comes along with being an actress is more of a struggle. Being an actress is a struggle; acting is not. The world "actress," the persona of it, hooks you onto some sort of responsibility to the press, which is a drag, especially at this time, right now.

WHY?

The time we are living in, this specific year, you don't see a lot of actors saying "fuck you" to the press in a cool way. Anybody can punch out a photographer—that doesn't take any energy at all. What takes energy is to say, "All right, you want it, you've got it," and after that I know you're going to leave me alone. The more you run away from the press, the more press you're going to get. It's so stupid.

WHAT ASPECT OF THE INDUSTRY HAS BEEN MOST DISAPPOINTING TO YOU?

I think it's a waste of money to spend $15 million on a movie about killing people. I think it's a bigger waste of money to spend $40 million on a movie about murder and revenge. I think it's much worse than sex. If shown in the right way, in a decent and loving way, sex is not a problem; it doesn't have to be dirty. I think it's dirtier to take your kids to see a movie about some big macho guy who goes around with a machine gun and blows people's brains out because of their political preference. I think it's sicker that people have bumper stickers on their car that say "Russia Sucks" than letting kids watch movies about love or watch other kids falling in love and making love. That is disappointing and infuriating to me. It's infuriating to me that films don't use their influence more. Films can do so much, and television can do even more, to make people aware of things. It's such a vast means of communication, and we don't use it to teach things that make people strong and real, and that is love and peace and forgiveness and honesty. I'd like to see that change; I'd like to do something about that. It's important to be able to contribute something positive.

WHAT ARE YOU DOING TO MAKE A DIFFERENCE?

I'm not involved in any organizations, but I have strong social values and strong responsibilities to this country and to this world. I feel like I have a responsibility to my fellow man and a responsibility to support what is right in my heart. That doesn't mean I am going to run for president. I think it is important to maintain strong social values, and we need to teach strong social values. I think it's important that we know what's right, and that killing and revenge are not the answer to world peace.

WHAT SPIRITUAL THINGS ARE IMPORTANT TO YOU?

I believe in God. I believe in karma, and that you reap what you sow. I've learned that from many other people I've met in my life and from books. I believe one should never stop giving; the more you give, the more you're getting at the same time. If you don't think about getting anything, it will come back to you—it's automatic. It's just there. That's why I'm in this business—I'm giving something. That's why it's so important to remember, acting in movies is not for my entertainment but rather for *other* people's entertainment. That's what I work 12 hours a day for, the enjoyment of the world. I want to bring happiness to the world.

WHAT IS YOUR BIGGEST FEAR?

My biggest fear is to stop learning and to stop wanting to go places. The minute I say, "I'm content; I think I'll stay here for the rest of my life," I'm dead. I won't even have to kill myself. I'll already be dead.

HOW DO YOU FEEL YOU FIT INTO THE CONTEXT OF *THE NEW BREED*?

I guess the way anybody does when they're getting to be successful. Hopefully, in 40 years, people will be writing about me in a book called *The Old Legends of Hollywood*. God knows.

Corey Feldman

WHAT WAS YOUR CHILDHOOD LIKE?

My childhood wasn't great, so it's not something I like talking about. I moved around a lot. I've been in the position of living in a broken-down, one-bedroom apartment without any furniture in a seedy area of Hollywood, but I've also been in the position of living in a $400,000 house with my entire family. Since I was three, I supported my family, so every time I worked more, we got a more expensive house.

WHAT WAS YOUR FAMILY LIKE? ARE YOUR PARENTS STILL TOGETHER?

No, they got divorced five or six years ago. First I lived with mom, then I lived with my grandmother, then I lived with mom again, then I lived with dad and now I'm emancipated. I've been through it all.

DID MOVING AROUND SO MUCH HAVE AN EFFECT ON YOU?

Definitely. I learned to grow and move past things normal people my age would not have done. I didn't get to goof around like most kids growing up.

HOW OLD ARE YOU?

I don't tell anyone my age; I won't even tell you off the record. I like to be very mysterious. Everything in my life has been like an open book, and I want to keep some things for myself. My age is something most people want to know, so I think it's one of the best things I can keep. It keeps people guessing.

DID YOU EVER HAVE A "NORMAL" FAMILY ENVIRONMENT?

Yes and no. We all lived together in a big house, but I always supported them; I always worked. What happened is, they

Until becoming an emancipated minor, Corey Feldman was lied to, manipulated, cheated, mismanaged and robbed blind by his mother and father. For 13 years, he worked as an actor, appearing in over 100 commercials, 50 guest spots on television series, three television series of his own and 12 feature films. Corey had earned over a million dollars, yet, because he was a minor, he never spent a penny of it.

He doesn't hate his parents for their greed, however, and he has chosen to move rather than dwell on the pain of the past. He feels his experiences have made him stronger and more determined. Corey's goal as an actor has always been to help people. The difference is, he has now amended that goal, and he is also beginning to help himself.

stole all my money and spent it. I didn't find out until it was too late, but when I was strong enough, I became emancipated. It took a long time because [my parents are] both conniving people. They would both sit there saying, "I'm sorry. I'm sorry. It will never happen again." I would go back to them, and they would do the same thing again. Finally, I just played them off one another until I could break free of them.

SO YOU'VE ALWAYS SUPPORTED YOUR FAMILY. WHAT WAS YOUR FIRST JOB AND HOW OLD WERE YOU?
I did a McDonald's commercial when I was three years old.

WHEN DID YOU DECIDE *YOU* WANTED TO BECOME AN ACTOR?
When I was about seven.

WHAT PROPELLED YOU TO THAT DECISION?
Because I knew my talent, and what I was doing was given to me by God. I feel I've been put on this planet with the abilities I have—I'm also a singer and dancer—to allow me to do what I'm doing. To help people, not only through my work, but also by bringing out public issues and writing back to people who write me letters. I try to reach out and help people—that's what I can give to the world. Acting takes people's pressures off of them; entertainment helps people relax and have fun. If there's anything I can do, I want to help, and God has given me my brains and my talent to do exactly that. I'm going to try my hardest to do it.

WHAT WERE YOUR GOALS WHEN YOU FIRST STARTED OUT AND HOW HAVE THEY CHANGED?
My goals have changed so many times. First I wanted anything, just to be on a TV series; then *I was* on a TV series. Then I wanted to star in a movie; well, I've starred in movies. Now, my goal—which is my final goal, I suppose, other than helping people—is to reach ultimate success and be bigger than Michael Jackson. To me, Michael Jackson is one of the biggest people to have ever lived as far as superstars go. What's weird is that we're friends, and he's been going since he was three and I've been going since I was three. He supported his family; I sup-

ported my family. There are a lot of similarities in our lives. My goal is to be at the position he's at when I'm 25.

HOW DO YOU FEEL ABOUT THE MAJORITY OF SCRIPTS YOU ARE SUBMITTED?
I had to wait a whole year, because the scripts I was getting after *Lost Boys* were no good, but you have to *wait* for perfection. In the past few months I've gotten three scripts, and I'm doing all three.

WHAT DO YOU LOOK FOR IN A SCRIPT?
Quality. Whether it's a comedy or a drama, I go for something that's going to further my career and not be a *detriment* to my career. I will not take anything where I would have to take my clothes off or where I would have to use the "F" word. I want to put out the best image, have the best reputation and be easy to work with. I want to be somebody people get along with and not somebody people are going to talk badly about. I don't care if other people are swearing or taking their clothes off—they can do anything they want to. I want my image, no matter what, to be clean. No one will be ever able to say, "Look at Corey Feldman—he's sitting there smoking and drinking and doing drugs in that movie." That's just not me.

WHEN YOU CONSIDER TAKING A ROLE, DO YOU THINK ABOUT WHAT EFFECT THE FILM WILL HAVE ON YOUR PEERS?
Sure. Mostly I consider what effect it's going to have on America, on the public. Recently, I've reached the point where a lot of people know who I am. I want to do everything possible to keep that in perspective so people don't start to think, "God, he's one of the bad people." I want them to think of me as one of the good people.

HOW DO YOU APPROACH A ROLE?
As delicately as possible.

WHAT KIND OF PREPARATION DO YOU DO?
I don't usually *do* preparation—I don't believe in it. I believe the best way to act is to be natural. That's my method. I don't believe in method acting. I don't believe in acting class; I think acting class is fine if you don't have a natural gift. Being that

I've never taken acting classes, I would never go to any acting class, and I would never suggest it to somebody. I feel if someone has the power inside of them to act, then they can do it themselves. They don't need to go to class; they just need to find themselves. I memorize my lines the night before, go to the set, get in front of the camera and, when the director says action, I start.

WHAT IS THE BIGGEST MISCONCEPTION ABOUT YOU?
There are a lot of misconceptions, and some of it has to do with the black. A lot of people think black is bad and that "I'm morbid because I wear it—which is completely the opposite of my feelings. Another misconception is that people think I'm involved with drugs, which I'm not at all—I'm completely against them. I used to do a lot of antidrug campaigns, but I don't want to do as much of that anymore, because I don't want to become too sugar-coated. I don't want to become Donny and Marie Osmond, because I'm not that. I'm not a bad person, but I'm not an angel either, by any means.

WHY DO YOU WEAR BLACK?
My reasons for wearing black is that black is always conceived of as being bad and morbid and dark and evil. I want people to know black is not a bad thing. People always take white as good and black as bad, whereas white is really the absence of all color and black is all colors combined. I wore black every day in 1987 as a symbol of anti-racism. I feel all races can live together. People think of black as bad because that's what was conceived in the olden days, and it's been passed down through the years. Maybe we don't have slavery anymore, but people—*ignorant* people—still hate blacks and they look at black colors and say that's bad, too—that it's morbid, depressing. That's not true.

IS BEING AN ACTOR EVER A STRUGGLE FOR YOU?
Yeah. I didn't work for a year, and that was a struggle. Then I shot four movies in a row; that's a struggle. I'm doing a record soon, and that's going to be a struggle, too, but I'm up for the challenge.

WHY ARE YOU ATTEMPTING A MUSIC CAREER AS WELL AS A FILM CAREER?

To me, music is a better way to communicate than movies because it's such a large audience. I performed at the Rose Bowl in front of 30,000 people—I loved it. I can't think of any bigger high in the world than hearing a mass of people cheering for you. Theater's too quiet; people can't get into it like they can at a concert. After these next four movies come out, I want to be known as a singer and dancer as much as an actor.

HOW DO YOU THINK YOUR IMAGE DIFFERS FROM YOU AS A PERSON?

I think people might conceive of me as tougher than I really am. I always play tough roles, but I'm really quiet, shy and innocent. A lot of my so-called friends make up rumors about me, telling other people things I would never do—drugs, sex, whatever. They mostly want to make me look cool, but what they don't realize is they're involving me in things I would never be involved in.

WHAT DO YOU LIKE BEST ABOUT SUCCESS?

That I can help people. I give a lot of money to charity, I do a lot of personal appearances, I do a lot of benefits.

WHAT IS YOUR BIGGEST DISAPPOINTMENT?

I don't have any. Even though I've had my bad times and my good times, I feel everything is moving at a steady pace, and the way God wants it to move. I'm not going to get impatient with it by regretting not doing this or that. I'm going to take things as they come.

WHAT SPIRITUAL THINGS ARE IMPORTANT TO YOU?

I don't believe in Jesus, Jehovah, Buddha or whatever. I know that there is a God; I don't know who He, She or Whatever it is. I know It's a being, and It's the most powerful being in the world. It has created everyone, and even though some people don't believe in Him, He doesn't hold it against them. He has His way of doing things and He plans your life. I don't need to go to church. The only relationship between me and God is that He knows I care. As long as He sees that people are caring, He's going to help them as much as He can. He may help them anyway. I don't know if there's a heaven or hell. I just know that I want to do things that feel right in my own heart. Things He would want me to do.

WHAT IS YOUR BIGGEST FEAR?

I wouldn't have any friends, people would stop listening to me and evil would take over the world.

IF TWO OTHER ACTORS WERE UP FOR THE SAME PART AS YOU, ALL THREE OF YOU WERE EQUAL IN TERMS OF LOOKS, TALENT, EXPERIENCE, ETC., WHY SHOULD THE DIRECTOR PICK YOU OVER THE OTHER TWO ACTORS?

Some actors are just in it for the money. Some actors are just in it for what they can get out of the whole Hollywood scene— that's the way a lot of people are in this town. I'm not into that. He should pick me because I'm doing what I've got to do and making the best quality work that's possible.

IF YOU HAD THREE WISHES, WHAT WOULD THEY BE?

I would wish for world peace, that no children would ever get hurt or killed again and that I would always do the best work I could possibly do.

WHAT SOCIAL ISSUES ARE IMPORTANT TO YOU?

Teen suicide.

HAVE YOU THOUGHT ABOUT COMMITTING SUICIDE AT ALL?

Sure. I've wanted to kill myself many times. I remember after my press conference on suicide, I wanted to commit suicide because of all the things that had gone wrong in my life. I've had so much hell in my life. You couldn't even compare it to most things.

WHAT STOPPED YOU?

I was scared—I couldn't do it. I know I'm too important to this world. I know there's too much for me to do. Why should I take my own life? God will take me when He's ready. I've fought too hard to overcome too many battles. Why should I throw it all away after fighting for so long. The only time I didn't think I was going to be able to go on was when it didn't look like I was going to get the emancipation. But I did, and I will go on. I'll never give up. I want to be around forever.

John Cusack

Growing up in an upper-middle-class neighborhood outside of Chicago, John Cusack never fit in. His intense feelings of alienation, combined with an overactive imagination, turned John into a problem child. His parents, distraught over his rebellious anti-establishment attitude and antics, encouraged him to vent his hostilities in a more positive, productive manner. John found the antidote to his frustrations in acting.

He joined a Chicago theater group run by friends of his parents. Surrounded by young people who shared and encouraged his creativity, John enjoyed peer acceptance for the first time in his life. When he was 16, he was cast in *Class*, but it was his comic vulnerability in Rob Reiner's *The Sure Thing* that earned him national notoriety.

Today, John splits his time between doing films and running the theater group he recently founded in Chicago.

DESCRIBE THE HOUSE AND NEIGHBORHOOD YOU GREW UP IN.

We lived in the finest suburb of Chicago, across the street from a park and a lake. I was a very lucky human being. My parents weren't unbelievably rich, but they had enough money when they started out to buy a house in a nice area. They went through a period where they had to scrape for the money to keep it. It was a white stucco house with a huge Christmas tree in the front.

HOW WOULD YOUR MOTHER DESCRIBE YOU AS A LITTLE KID?

I was lazy and only interested in doing the things that interested me. I still am kind of. I've never had the discipline to do things the way other people do.

IF I WERE TO ASK ONE OF YOUR FRIENDS FROM HIGH SCHOOL WHAT YOU WERE LIKE, WHAT WOULD THEY SAY AND HOW WOULD THEY DESCRIBE YOU?

I was very anti-high school—I didn't get along with that institution at all. I hated high school with a passion.

DID YOU CUT SCHOOL A LOT?

Oh, I cut as much as I could to remain a B−/C+ student; my parents would have raised hell if I didn't get decent grades. I started out going to public school, but in junior high school I created an alternate way of living, which is a very strange thing for a boy who's in sixth grade to do. It was called "Jo Mania."

WHAT WAS "JO MANIA"?

It was a kind of anarchy gibberish code that me and a couple of other sick little monsters thought up—a series of non-sequential abstract paragraphs that we would spew at people. We thought it was the funniest thing. We'd call up radio shows till 5 or 6 a.m. on school nights and talk about Ed Asner eating corn; we'd tape it and play it back. So I spent most of my time spewing gibberish as a child. The more abstract it got, the harder we'd laugh—we'd laugh ourselves into crying fits. My parents were concerned, which is understandable, so they sent me to Catholic school.

WHEN DID YOU DECIDE YOU WANTED TO BECOME AN ACTOR?

That's strange. I think people fall into act-ing. Someone asks me, "Should I be an actor?" I say, "I don't know man, proba-bly not." The people I know who are good actors are social-psychological mutants in a way because they're shy and intro-verted. They have such a need to express themselves; if they don't, they may ex-plode. They're not regular people who are happy with just being themselves and with the ordinary pleasures of life. They have a much deeper need to be accepted and a vitality to them to which I relate.

WHAT WAS YOUR FIRST ROLE?

When I was 10, I joined a theater group owned by friends of my parents called the Pivot Theater Workshop. We did a lot of improvisations. We'd take short stories by authors like Salinger and Bradbury and adapt them. Aidan Quinn, Rosanna Ar-quette and a lot of people who've started to work in theater and films were trained there.

WHAT WAS YOUR FIRST PROFESSIONAL ROLE?

I sometimes wonder why, at 13, I had this drive to be in film, why I wasn't content to play. When I was 14, I did two industrial films—I got 700 bucks for each. In the first one, I played a city boy who goes to the country and discovers the wonders of dairy products. I went to a farm and met my cousin Tracy. My Uncle Jim was there, and we talked about dairy products. It just doesn't seem right to me that I was doing that, but, um, you know, so be it. In the second one I played a problem child.

Then I did some commercials. I did one for Nightlight. My line was, "Look, flick this switch, it's a flashlight; flick this switch it's a wild strobe." You tell me—was I some fucker, or what?

WHAT WERE YOUR GOALS WHEN YOU FIRST STARTED OUT AND HOW HAVE THEY CHANGED?

I started out saying, "I want to do roles in films." I could have been motivated—no, I probably *was* motivated—by jealousy from other people, wanting attention, and just drive and ambition, because I did think I could do it. All those feelings are tied together. When I was eight, I had this weird pragmatism that I knew I couldn't be a football player, but I thought, "I can act; yeah, sure I can bullshit." That's what I thought it was in a way—bullshit. Then I got hooked up with people in a very good theater group who had a love for acting and who taught me respect for it.

When I was 16, I walked into my agent's office in Chicago, [the Ann Geddes agency], and I said, "If you'll get me an audition, I'll get the part." I was just a real cocky 16-year-old kid. The next day she sent me out for *Class*, and I got the part.

WHAT ARE YOUR GOALS TODAY?

To do no more bad films, that's my goal. If I do a film, it has to be anything from good to great, or something that at least has the guts to *risk* for good-to-great.

WHAT DO YOU LOOK FOR IN A SCRIPT?

That's been changing. Most of the scripts I get are trash. One of the things that got me in trouble, I think, was that I thought I could fix holes in scripts by improvising cool lines or coming up with stuff. What I learned was that the holes don't fix them-selves. You have to start with a good script. You have to look for something that's structurally sound and which is also *about* something—that has some mes-sage you either agree with or you don't agree with, but is interesting regardless. That's what I look for now. Also, I'd like to work with great directors like Alan Parker, Stanley Kubrick and Woody Allen.

YOU'VE ALREADY WORKED WITH WONDERFUL DIRECTORS LIKE ROB REINER AND JOHN SAYLES.

Those guys are the two opposite sides of the spectrum as directors. Reiner gets as excited and passionate as you do and makes you match that passion right there with him. Sayles gives you a strange kind of disconnected support and strength and just kind of lets you do what you want. They're both effective, but they come from different angles.

WHAT KINDS OF ROLES ARE YOU LOOKING FOR?

I'd rather not do any more films where I fall in love with a girl, because I feel I keep doing that. I keep doing that and graduat-ing from high school—my dream and my nightmare. The other day I read this script which was really well-written; it was a love story, and I said to myself: "Fuck, man, I don't care. I'll do anything as long as it's good." The most important thing is to be in a good director's film, be part of a clear vision and fucking *foam* for him—work as hard as I can. When I worked for Reiner, I think I put so much of myself into my character at the end of the day, I was really tired and felt I couldn't have done any better. I probably could have, but I felt, "Shit, man, at least I worked my ass off; at least I gave it all I had that day." I wish I felt that way about every film. Some directors are just not as competent as they would lead you to believe.

HAVE YOU HAD ANY BAD EXPERIENCES?

I think everything is probably going the way it should go. I have a good understanding now of what's good. Over the past two years I've learned a lot about the business—from the time I did *The Sure Thing* until now. At first I thought I didn't have to worry about it because I'd be able to pick out all the bullshit.

LIKE WHAT?

You have all these slimy fucks coming at you from different directions—agents, producers and directors who are real good at meeting you in the office, but when you get out on a set, they're not half as good. They talk a good game, but they don't produce.

I've done all these films and made all this money, but I've been really depressed after a lot of them came out—it really fucked me up. No one seems to want to hear that it's hard. Sure, you make a lot of money, but if you care about what you do and have pride, you *hurt* when it doesn't turn out to be good.

WHY DO YOU STILL LIVE IN CHICAGO?

I like the snow. I like wearing a nice overcoat—I like the look. I like fires and being with my family and the friends I grew up around Christmas time. I like to drink, hang out, whatever. I like to go out and meet people who are not in "the business"; you can do that here. You go out in L.A. and you only meet actresses and people with scripts.

SO YOU CONSIDER CHICAGO TO BE YOUR HOME?

For now it is.

IS STUDYING IMPORTANT FOR YOUR GROWTH AS AN ACTOR?

I think studying things *other* than acting is important for me to grow as an actor. When I went to NYU, I took a law class and an ethics class. For me, the more I grow as a person, the more I learn about new things and meet cool people with good visions and ideas, the cooler I'll be on film and onstage.

WHAT HAS BEEN YOUR GREATEST SACRIFICE FOR SUCCESS?

I don't know; I don't know if I'm really successful. I think I've made some money, and I think people recognize me sometimes, but I don't think I'm *that* successful. The only thing, on a smaller scale, is when people who don't know you come up to you and want to be a part of your life. By them actually seeing you, it makes them feel better, so it's a weird kind of responsibility and you try to be courteous. I'm trying to proceed with my life—do films, see my family, work with my theater company, try to find another girlfriend—and these people want to talk to you about your films and, "What do you think about this?" It gets kind of tiring after a while.

HOW DOES YOUR ONSCREEN IMAGE DIFFER FROM YOU AS A PERSON?

I don't know. I haven't even seen some of the films I've been in. I never saw *In Hot Pursuit* or *One Crazy Summer*; I knew I wouldn't be happy with myself or my performance.

BUT FROM THE FILMS YOU HAVE SEEN, IS YOUR PERSONA ONSCREEN SIMILAR TO YOUR PERSONA OFFSCREEN?

Yeah. There was a lot of me in *The Sure Thing*. I just try to go in there and make the moment real; I try to make that connection and be spontaneous. When I do a role, I bring a lot of myself into it, but I also take on the characterization of that character. You become the characters you play, more than you even know. I did a film called *Tapeheads* where I got the chance to play this sleazy white-trash would-be video producer, whose only assets are his loyalty to his friends and this kind of success drive. When I was doing that film, I started talking like him and taking on a lot of his characteristics. I found myself talking to women in clubs saying ridiculous things; it was great.

DOES IT TAKE YOU A LONG TIME TO RECOVER FROM A PART?

When you do a film, especially one you feel has a good chance of being good, you go boom-boom-boom for 12 weeks, hauling ass, trying to make everything work. When you finish it, you look around and there's nothing to do- the rest of your life can't possibly be as exciting and as stimulating as those 12 manic weeks you spent with this new group of people. On a set, you become a family, you have affairs and you do all of these incredible things— your regular life can't possibly match up to it. For a couple of days afterwards, I sit around, drink beer and stare at the walls; there is kind of a letdown.

IS BEING AN ACTOR EVER A STRUGGLE FOR YOU?

Sure. Every time I take a role, I wonder if I'm going to be good. I think, "Am I going to be right for this? Am I concentrating as much as I can?" The other struggle is dealing with the fine line between me and the spirit of partying. Part of working on a film is getting together and enjoying people and sharing a commitment to what you're doing, getting really wild and sick, having fun and laughing a lot. When you're doing a film, though, there are only so many hours in a day, and there's a fine line between partying to get you into the right mood to jam together on a film, and abusing it by just partying too much.

WHO ARE SOME OF YOUR IDOLS OR PEOPLE YOU RESPECT?

I've never had this image of myself being like a James Dean or a Marlon Brando. Actors I relate to are guys like Dustin Hoffman and Jimmy Stewart, who aren't unbelievably into being these introverted superstuds. They're into being as honest and passionate about their work as they can, trying to give the roles they do some life and truth.

WHAT'S YOUR BIGGEST FEAR?

I have many of them, but my biggest one is that I'll waste my potential.

HOW DO YOU FEEL YOU FIT INTO THE CONTEXT OF THE NEW BREED?

If you recognize that I'm a good actor, hard-working and trying to be in better projects, that's probably how I fit into the new breed. All I can say is that I will do better work in the next ten years, because that's what I want to do.

Jennifer Rubin

The desert is very hot, and the air is very still. Within the stillness and quiet, everything has its own specific place. Like my family, it is a very strict environment that carries its own set of rules. In our house, that included making sure the carpet stood up in a certain direction at all times.

Until high school, we lived in a trailer park in Arizona. I had to be inside before dark. At night I'd just sit in my hot, stuffy room, thinking and being quiet. My mother was an alcoholic. By the time she was twenty-four, she had four kids; she drank because she didn't know how else to deal with her frustrations. She worked a day job and a night job as a medical transcriptionist. When she got home, there was to be no noise.

The ground inside the trailer was hollow, so we had to walk lightly. I shared a bunkbed with my little brother, my two older sisters shared the other bedroom. Sometimes he'd put on shows. He'd be Lola the showgirl. My brother has black eyes, and I'd try to find his pupils all the time. He'd make faces, and I'd sit there and crack up— quietly.

I thought I was Billie Holiday— poor little white girl. She was from the ghetto and I was from the dirt. I had that same desire to be better. I signed all my high school yearbooks, "See you in the movies." I had take drama class, but deep down I never really thought I was going to leave Arizona.

That all changed when Billy Ford from the Ford Agency saw me walking at the University of Arizona; I was visiting my sister at the time. He flew me to New York City, and I immediately started working as a model. Modeling is not like acting— you don't work up to anything. You start working the first day, because your time clock is ticking. It was culture shock, and that's when I became wild.

I don't want to say I was a model, because I wasn't a successful model; you have to think you are

pretty to model. I think there is a beauty deep inside of me, but I don't think my body and looks are where my greatest beauty lies. It became a big problem because I thought that way.

I was living out my Billy Holiday fantasy. The drugs, the chic, the rich men—all of that. I didn't fuck, though, so that was another problem. Rich men want to fuck you instead of making love to you or thinking you can be their girlfriend; girls do that. I went through a lot of shit, and I had a lot of people to deal with, in an uneducated, un- skilled way. No matter what obstacles I faced, though, I knew I'd end up doing the work I wanted to do.

Finally I just couldn't deal with it anymore. I saw a girl on a Club Med poster, sitting alone on the beach, and that day I packed my bags and ended up on an island without any phones for three months. My mother finally found me and asked me to come home. I went home for a few days and then I moved to Los Angeles to study acting.

This time, however, I was starting out differently—I had money. I wanted to learn from a great teacher. I would hear about a dif- ferent great teacher almost every week, though, so I ended up study- ing with almost every acting teacher in Los Angeles. I learned that there are not a lot of great teachers out there, for me. Maybe a lot of those teachers had good ad- vice for me, but after a while I just stopped listening to them—I wasn't in the space to apply it. I made the decision to act on how I feel.

Through a casting agent, I got an appointment with Sandy Bresler and John Kelly. When they signed me, I had no idea they were the creme de la creme of Hollywood. At the time, they only represented Jack Nicholson and 12 other clients. It gave me instant credibility.

My first role as an actress was on the *Twilight Zone*. I played a girl who had an unreasonably strict fa- ther. I fell in love with a boy and turned into a wolf so we could be together forever. I had a lot of experience to draw on for that part. Since then I've looked for strong women's roles, but it's been tough to find them. There's a shortage of these parts. The reason? Hollywood is, now and forever, a man's town. The men control the money and properties, and as a result, women are usually the victims. The only difference now is that more films are featuring women's transitions, as opposed to just men's.

When I do accept a role, I read and I research until I feel that, no matter what I do and what I say, I'm that character. That's only really happened to me once, though—with *Permanent Record*. As Sean Penn puts it, I got into my cage. "Cage" is that moment when I realized I've done everything I can do, where there is not an action or a word that my character would not do. Not every role requires a cage. For *Bad Dreams*, a sci-fi horror flick about manipulation and incest, I didn't need to prepare—I just did it. So in that sense, the preparation varies.

I have a lot of pain and emotion inside of me; for me, that is the only thing there is. I'm not a classical actress—I'm from the street. I don't know anything else but how and what I feel. For that reason, I would go through all that I've gone through again. That struggle is kind of beautiful. People like to take the struggle out of life, but I don't know why they try to deny themselves that experience—it makes you stronger and appreciate things more.

Acting is the only honest living I know. When people see my work, they are going to say, "Jennifer Rubin is like a really heavy chick," but I'm not. I have a lot of crazy, joking good fun in life, but in character, I am one heavy chick. I take life lightly, but I don't take life lightly onscreen.

Corey Haim

WHAT WAS LIFE LIKE BEFORE YOU BECAME AN ACTOR?

I was a kid who went to school and hung out with my friends. I was little mommy's and daddy's boy; I went out with them all the time, and we were one big happy family. When we moved to Los Angeles, my parents got divorced, my sister moved back to Toronto to finish school and my dad moved to Montreal. My mom and I are the last survivors of the Haim family. We fight a lot, but we're a team. She looks after me and supports me in my work. I don't hang out with her that much, though. I'm out all the time with my girlfriend and my friends; I'm just my own person now.

HOW WOULD YOUR MOTHER DESCRIBE YOU AS A LITTLE KID?

A little terror.

WHEN DID YOU DECIDE TO BECOME AN ACTOR?

When I was ten years old. My sister and I had a couple of friends who did commercials. We wanted to do that, so we did and that was that. It looked like fun being on TV around celebrities. I thought it would be kind of cool.

WHAT WAS YOUR FIRST ROLE AS AN ACTOR?

The first thing I ever did was a commercial for Sears, but my first acting role was on a show called *The Edison Twins*. It was about a brother, sister and a younger brother who play detectives; I played the younger brother. My first movie role was *First Born* with Terri Garr. I've done nine movies since then.

HOW DO YOU FEEL ABOUT THE MAJORITY OF SCRIPTS SENT TO YOU?

They're not very good. There are too many politics in the film business. Say there's a successful film about a cat and a dog fighting, and the cat takes out his claws and swipes the dog's nose. I'll get another script a few months later where there's a cat and a rat fighting and the cat takes its tail and swats the rat in the head

Nothing in the world is more important to Corey Haim than being cool; the dude has it down to a science. Corey believes coolness is something that starts deep within your soul and manifests itself materially in things like the car you drive, the clothes you wear, who you hang out with and, most importantly, who your girlfriend is and what she looks like.

If it sounds like beneath Corey's surface lies more surface, bear in mind he's fifteen and a half (accent stressed on the "half"). Like most kids his age, he can't wait to get his driver's license, he adores his mother (whom he calls Judy), he is madly in love (and feels love knows no age barriers) and he spends too much money on bubble gum and comic books. The possible similarities between Corey and his peers end about there, however.

For the past four years, Corey has been working steadily as an actor, commanding big bucks and choice roles. His roles include a haunting performance as the sensitive courageous nerd in *Lucas*, and as the younger brother of Jason Patric in *The Lost Boys*. Although he may come off as flip, crazy or carefree, work comes first for him. Corey has sacrificed his teenage years for a successful acting career, surrounding himself with a team on managers, agents and publicists to help him reach his personal goal—winning an Academy Award.

or something. It's kind of the same thing. There are too many scripts that are saying the same thing. There's no real imagination now days.

WHAT DO YOU LOOK FOR IN A SCRIPT?
Entertainment. Pure nonstop entertainment.

WHEN YOU GET A PART, HOW DO YOU APPROACH A ROLE?
I just kind of get into it. In *Lucas*, I had to do a lot of preparation, though. I had to play a nerd, and that was really hard for me; it's so far removed from my personality. I had to key down a lot. A few minutes before we'd do each take, I'd have to get into my own world and become Lucas. I don't like playing nerdy characters.

WAS FINDING THE RIGHT AGENT

DIFFICULT?
No. After I did *First Born*, the producer, Stanley Jaffe, called an agent named Vicki Light and said, "I've got this new up-and-coming kid; I want you to take him as a client." She said, "No problem Mr. Jaffe, sir," and she took me as a client. Easy.

WHAT HAS BEEN YOUR BIGGEST SACRIFICE FOR SUCCESS?
Moving from Toronto to Los Angeles. It's a 3,000-mile move, and we did it. It's not like I can just pick up and go back on a whim. I'm not saying I *want* to go back; I'm just saying I couldn't even if I wanted to. We've started life over here.

DO YOU FEEL YOU'RE MISSING OUT ON YOUR TEENAGE YEARS AT ALL?
Yeah, but you only live once, and this was meant to be, I guess. I kind of feel like I'm

exchanging one thing for another. I'm just taking life as it comes.

WHAT IS THE BIGGEST MISCONCEPTION ABOUT YOU?
People think I have a really weak personality—not into life, tired, kind of apathetic. I'm really hyper, outgoing and fun. I just don't show that side of me much to the public. I only do it when it's needed.

HOW DOES YOUR IMAGE DIFFER FROM YOU AS A PERSON?
One is Corey Haim the actor; the other, Corey Haim the person. Corey Haim the actor is someone who knows a lot of people in the industry and has to be like, "Hi, how are you?" *kiss kiss*, and have an extra-nice-boy attitude. If you do the slightest thing wrong, normal people will just say, "Oh, he's just a person," but people in the entertainment business

would freak out and say, "Oh, can you believe Corey Haim did this or this?" When it really doesn't matter, and it wasn't anything major. Corey Haim the person doesn't care about having to be extra nice; he just is who he is.

WHAT DO YOU LIKE BEST ABOUT SUCCESS?

The PR. It's kind of fun; it's cool. All the people know who you are and appreciate your work.

IF YOU COULD DO AN ONSCREEN BIOGRAPHY OF ANYONE IN HISTORY, WHO WOULD IT BE AND WHY?

John Ritter. The man has a certain class about himself. He's a real actor; he knows exactly what he's doing. He has good feelings about a lot of things. He's been my idol forever, ever since I saw *Three's Company*. He's unbelievable.

DO YOU HAVE ANY OTHER IDOLS?

Mel Gibson. He's a great actor; he's very cool.

WHAT'S *COOL* TO YOU? DEFINE IT.

You can't. What's cool? Hip. What's hip? Very hip; modern. What's modern? See, you can't. *Cool* is Mel Gibson, so if you want to know what *cool* is, go see Mel Gibson.

IS BEING COOL IMPORTANT TO YOU?

Being cool is the most important thing. If you lose your cool, to me, you lose everything. If you lose your cool, you become weak, and when you're weak, you lose it all.

IS COOL SOMETHING OUTSIDE OF YOU OR IS IT ON THE INSIDE?

Both. You have to go inside to bring it out. If you're cool inside, and you know you're cool inside, then you can kind of be that without looking egotistical. You can do it in a way that people will say, "Oh, he's cool, but he just doesn't like showing it."

HOW DO YOU, COREY HAIM, BRING YOUR COOLNESS OUT FROM WITHIN AND EXTERNALIZE IT?

I just do. The way I dress, the car I just bought, the girl I go out with . . . and that's *girl*, not *girls*—that's something

right there. I'm not into girls, I'm into a girl. It's all in the way I conduct myself.

WHAT KIND OF MOVIES MAKE YOU LAUGH?

Young Frankenstein. Comedies with a drama kick to them. *The Rocky Horror Picture Show*.

WHAT KIND OF MOVIES MAKE YOU CRY?

None. I never cry in movies, for some reason. The only movie I've ever cried in was *ET*, and that was ages ago.

IS CRYING NOT COOL?

Crying is *very* cool. Crying is actually one of the coolest things you can do.

WHAT SPIRITUAL THINGS ARE IMPORTANT TO YOU?

Crystals. I'm very into crystals. They mean a lot.

WHAT DO THEY MEAN?

Instead of saying "knock on wood," why not say "knock on crystal." There's so much more talk about crystals. They have power and energy.

WHAT IS YOUR BIGGEST FEAR?

Death. The fear of not being here and talking to you right now. The fear of leaving here, going to work at 12:30, sneaking over to my girlfriend's house and getting back to work without getting caught. The fear of not having the knowledge to bring myself back. You never experience death until you're dead, and that's what's so scary about it.

WHAT DO YOU THINK HAPPENS TO YOU AFTER YOU DIE?

You go into nothingness. You don't think, you don't talk, you don't breathe, you don't move—you're just a thought in the air, a memory, something that kicks in once in a while and then kicks out. The concept of death frightens me.

WHAT ARE SOME OF YOUR VICES?

I don't drink or do drugs or anything like that. They lead to death, and death is scary, man—death scares the shit out of me. What happens if you do a drug one night and it's laced with something. You freak out and—boom—you die. I've experienced drinking and smoking pot, but never again. It's a bad thing to drink; it's a

worse thing to do drugs.

DO YOU MANAGE YOUR MONEY WELL?

No. I'm still 15. I buy synthesizers and clothes and lottery tickets and Archie comics and bubble gum. I can spend $50 on gum and comics without even noticing it. It's so stupid.

WHO IS THE IDEAL LEADING LADY YOU COULD BE CAST OPPOSITE?

Her name is La La; she's my girlfriend right now. One night me and her were at this hotel called Paradise. We sat in front of a mirror and we were kissing. We watched ourselves kiss in the mirror. It's kind of funny because when you're with a person for a long period of time, you both hook into one, and both of you are totally comfortable with anything you do or how you do it. When we were watching ourselves kiss, it looked perfect.

IF THERE WERE TWO OTHER ACTORS UP FOR THE SAME PART AS YOU, AND ALL THREE WERE TOTALLY EQUAL IN TERMS OF LOOKS, TALENT, ETC., WHY SHOULD A DIRECTOR CHOOSE YOU OVER THE OTHER TWO CHARACTERS?

Kirk Cameron, River Phoenix and myself?

OK.

I have a certain quality about myself that, when it comes down to acting, I'm involved in every way. I try to be helpful and give my ideas. No one has ever really tapped my potential yet, though. *Lucas* was not even close. I don't know what the part is that will show my talent off, but it's out there somewhere for me.

WHAT SOCIAL ISSUES ARE IMPORTANT TO YOU?

None. If you get on the bandwagon, you get ragged on. People say, "Oh, he's not really meaning what he says; he's just doing it for the publicity." So if I don't mean it, why should I do it?

HOW DO YOU FIT INTO THE CONTEXT OF THE NEW BREED?

I have a rawness about myself. I hope I make it, but if I don't, I'll just get back to life as it was in Toronto. I'm not really worried about it, and besides, I'm cool.

Elizabeth Perkins

When Elizabeth Perkins feels threatened or gets insecure, she says she overcompensates by becoming arrogant. Beneath the "little walls and eggshells" she builds up to protect herself, however, lies the same vulnerable, sensitive girl from Vermont, who turned to acting because she felt she couldn't effectively express herself in the "normal sense of society's ideals," and sought a more creative outlet.

For Elizabeth, acting was not only a way to step out of herself, but also a way to step *into* herself. Her work continues to function as a constant catharsis for her life, the only difference being she now connects herself to a role instead of inventing someone else, thus bringing herself into the piece. Elizabeth says she lives for the moments when she loses herself in the work and is truly set free.

WHAT DO YOU REMEMBER ABOUT GROWING UP IN VERMONT?

I remember lots of dirt roads and cow pastures. I remember the smell of dried grass, gasoline, clean air, wet dogs and chicken shit. I remember there being lots of laughter and dead silence.

HOW WOULD YOUR MOTHER DESCRIBE YOU AS A LITTLE KID?

I think she would say I was very introspective while being very extroverted. She would say I was a loner because I was always playing by myself—and more like a boy than a girl. I didn't do things that little girls did, I did things that little boys did: I went hunting and fishing, I didn't wear a shirt in the summer, I didn't have dolls, I caught frogs and killed squirrels, I drove snowmobiles around and I started smoking cigarettes at a very young age. I've always felt more comfortable around men.

IF I WERE TO ASK ONE OF YOUR FRIENDS FROM HIGH SCHOOL WHAT YOU WERE LIKE, WHAT WOULD THEY SAY?

They'd say I was a troublemaker and a stoner. I ran into somebody whose cousin was a girl who knew me in high school. She described me as a vandal and a thief, and that's pretty much what I was. I didn't really fit in; I was odd. I think I knew from a very early age that school wasn't where I wanted to be, and I wasn't going to learn what I wanted to do in a classroom. I always felt like I was there because it was the law. I didn't really accept that very well—I've always had a problem with authority. I think I started to get high at a young age because it took me to more places than school ever could. Now I'm clean and sober, which is one of the best feelings in the world, but I'm learning a lot every day.

WHAT WAS YOUR FIRST ROLE?

Hansel. I was auditioning for Gretel, and they said, "We enjoyed your Gretel, but we were wondering if you'd be interested in playing Hansel," so I did that.

WHAT WAS YOUR FIRST PROFESSIONAL ROLE?

My first experience when I really knew I was going to be an actress was after I got out of school. I studied for a few years at the Goodman Theater in Chicago, but I think it was more of a hobby at that point, not something that I was dead-serious about. I was cast in a play called "Gardenia" by John Guare, and it changed my life. This play was poetry and beautifully written, wonderfully staged—and the director took us through an experience that drew us together like a family. From then on, the stage and the people in the theater really became like a family to me, and that was wonderful, because I never had much of a family.

WHAT WERE YOUR GOALS THEN AND HOW HAVE THEY CHANGED NOW?

I think everybody's goals change from day to day. I've stopped trying to set goals for myself, because I think I have too many expectations for myself that I can never live up to—they just put me in a bad place. I'm now at the stage where I'm trying to experience things as they happen instead of trying to *make* them happen. I know I'd like to work, but it's also not my main priority for being in this world.

WHAT *IS* YOUR MAIN PRIORITY?

To be happy and enjoy life. When I started out, career moves were very important to me. I had to let that go because it doesn't become about the work, it becomes about climbing up the ladder; I don't want to get lost in that. I think my goals are to work with people I respect, to have relationships with people I respect and to respect myself. I don't have a goal to win an award or be in a best picture of the year. I can't think that way—I'd just get screwed up.

WHAT DO YOU LOOK FOR IN A SCRIPT?

In the beginning I used to read "the part," and that's really changed for me. Now I look to see if the script has a good beginning, middle and end. You can read a script that has a good beginning and a good middle, but you rarely have one that is tied together at the end. I look to see what changes all the characters go through, and almost last, I look to see how much my character goes through. I think that most screenplays originally written as stageplays turn out better, because most stage plays have climaxes, motivating forces and all the stuff the masters talk about, which is missing from a lot of screenplays. When you look at screenplays' breakdowns and treatments, they start them out as scenes rather than pieces. With a play, scenes are written as an arc.

IS IT IMPORTANT TO BALANCE YOUR FILM CAREER WITH THEATER?

Yes. I recently turned down a play simply because I had just finished a film and I wasn't ready to go back to work—but I want to do a play soon. I think to go back and do a stageplay now, though, it would have to be a piece I really felt I *had* to do. I'm sort of like that with film now, too. I've gotten my foot in the door, and now, hopefully, I can be very selective.

WHAT KINDS OF ROLES ARE YOU LOOKING FOR?

I've always found if you look for something, you don't get it—kind of like if you're looking for love, love's not going to find you. Any actress looks for a role she can bring to life, that touches a part of her. I think I look for roles that will let me touch a new part of myself, that I'll learn something from and I'll grow from somehow. If I read a script and feel I can't do a part, then I *want* to do it. If I read it and it kind of scares me, then I know I should pursue it.

HOW DO YOU APPROACH AND PREPARE FOR A ROLE?

My approaches to stage and film are very different. With a play, you have eight hours a day to work on your role, and you grow through the other actors, the director and the staging. You live with it for a month before you perform it; you have the chance to discover things and you have the luxury of time to break down the script and write about your character.

For a film, I think it requires much more of a solitary effort. Unfortunately, we are not usually afforded the opportunity to be part of the collaborative effort—our opinion comes somewhere between the key grip's and the best boy's, which is unfortunate in a lot of cases. Unless you're in-volved from pre-production to post-production, you don't really have much control. I spend time at home—not to make concrete choices, but leave avenues open for choice. There's nothing worse than making a choice in your living room and bringing it to the set, because it never works. If you're lucky, you get to work with a costar who is willing to give and take; that is also rare.

WHEN YOU ACCEPT A PART, DO YOU CONSIDER WHAT EFFECT YOUR ROLE WILL HAVE ON PEOPLE?

I don't think so, because then I'd be doing it for somebody other than myself, and I can't look at it that way. I worked with an actor once who said in discussing a scene with a director, "Oh, but the audience will love it." I can't think that way because, it's not for what I'm going to learn, it's for effect—and then it's dishonest manipulation. Everybody likes to be enjoyed. Everybody likes people to go to their plays or films and walk away with something, but you can't gauge what they're going to get out of what you do—and if you're doing something to gauge what somebody's going to feel, then I think you're doing it for all the wrong reasons. I have a desire to express myself to an audience, but I'm not responsible for the way an audience reacts. It's kind of like if a sculptor sculpts something so he'll get a good reception at the gallery. Is he doing what he wants? Is that making him feel better?

WHAT HAS BEEN YOUR BIGGEST SACRIFICE FOR SUCCESS?

Normalcy. Actors don't live lives like other people live. We don't get up in the morning like normal people, we don't go to bed at night like normal people; we don't eat like them, drink like them, we don't sleep like them. Actors are a breed apart, and sometimes there are moments when I wish I worked in a bank, just to feel what it would be like to come home and watch *Three's Company*—just to see if I could fit in. When you work on a film, you don't have the time to have coffee with friends on Saturday afternoon, go to dinner parties or go bowling. You miss out on a lot of middle-class life, and sometimes I think it would be nice to live like a normal person.

IS BEING AN ACTRESS EVER A STRUGGLE FOR YOU?

No. I have a hard time with the "tortured actor" thing, because anyone who makes a living as an actor has very little to complain about. We have more freedom than most people in the world to do what we want and to be able to support ourselves and live the lifestyle we create. It's a gift—don't think I don't recognize that. I know what I have and I feel fortunate to have it.

WHAT DO YOU LIKE BEST ABOUT SUCCESS?

I don't have to wait on tables anymore. I have the freedom to grow and to do the things I want to do. It's unfortunate in a lot of ways that only through success can an actor do what he really wants to do.

WHAT IS YOUR BIGGEST DISAPPOINTMENT UP TO THIS POINT?

That my faith isn't stronger. I think I judge myself a lot, and I'd always hoped by that time I reached 27, I would have more faith in myself and those around me. I think that's what I'm striving for now. I get disappointed with myself; I get disappointed with my spirituality.

WHAT SPIRITUAL THINGS ARE IMPORTANT TO YOU?

Acceptance, unconditional love, hope, being open, trusting. I get lost in all of those things a lot. Louise Hay taught me a lot. I used her meditation tape every night for a year and read her books.

WHAT IS YOUR BIGGEST FEAR?

Judgment. Not people judging me so much as me judging other people. I fear my own resentments and judgments the most. People can do things I don't like and I can take them in or let them go. I fear what my own brain can do to me.

HOW DO YOU FEEL YOU FIT INTO THE CONTEXT OF THE NEW BREED?

I think the age of pretty boys and pretty girls has fallen by the wayside. When I look at myself in terms of the way the business looks at me, I have sort of a funny face—it's kind of off-center. I'm not extremely beautiful, I'm not the girl next door and I'm not extremely marketable. I don't fit in. What I *do* possess, however, is a sense of honesty. I don't come out with a mask on like Joan Collins. I'm willing to show myself.

Esai Morales

"Affection is the ridiculous effort of the ignorant to appear wise, the attempt of the barren soul to appear rich."

The Urantia Book

Another hot summer night in New York's South Bronx. The air is thick with grime and pollution, and the humidity is so high, your clothes cling to your skin with sweat the moment you step out into the street. Tempers rise with the temperature as the rhythm of the city approaches its usual frenetic pace.

The streets are alive. Old women sit perched in their window seats like society ladies in their boxes at the opera, watching the drama unfold, waiting for something to happen. Mothers, cradling crying babies in their arms, call for their children in Spanish, Chinese, Korean and myriad other languages. You don't hear much English in this part of town.

The children, ignoring their mothers, continue to run through the cool spray of water jetting out of an open fire hydrant, breakdancing to the sounds pulsating out of their bombastic boom boxes and getting high with their older brothers and sisters. The older children hold fort in an abandoned building. The scent of sex, sweat and marijuana lingers in the air. Soon _they_ will have babies to contend with, but for now, these kids have no concerns aside from getting high, getting laid and protecting their territory.

Their fathers seem oblivious to everything around them. They sit in front of the corner bodega, playing cards and drinking tequila and beer, hoping they get lucky on the bets they placed with their bookies that afternoon. Their only concern seems to be to stay cool—both physically and emotionally.

And so it is, day after day, month after month, season after season, year after year. The only things that change are the faces.

Esai Morales knew he was different. He knew he had to get out of the South Bronx. From a very young age he knew he possessed a special gift—the ability to entertain people and make them laugh.

At the High School for the Performing Arts in New York City, Esai successfully transformed his gift into a craft. After graduation he was cast opposite Sean Penn in _Bad Boys_. Although his career has had its ups and downs since then, Esai has been able to use his craft to transcend the harsh realities of the Bronx.

Today, he commutes between his apartment on Manhattan's Upper East Side and his home in West Hollywood, California. He has not forgotten his roots, however, and he intends to use his position as an actor to improve the quality of the image Americans have of Hispanics. Esai considers himself a pupil as well as a teacher and says his main goal as an actor is to make a difference.

HOW WOULD YOUR MOTHER DESCRIBE YOU AS A CHILD?

She would say I was a very good boy when I was sleeping. I was a terror. I never stopped asking questions. I never stopped taking things apart and trying to put them back together. My mother was an organizer for the ladies' garment union. One of my earliest memories was eavesdropping on her conversations with her co-workers, telling them not to take the abuse of their boyfriends or husbands. I don't remember my father and mother ever being together. She left him when I was two. Respect was the one thing she taught me. Inadvertently, it backfired on her during

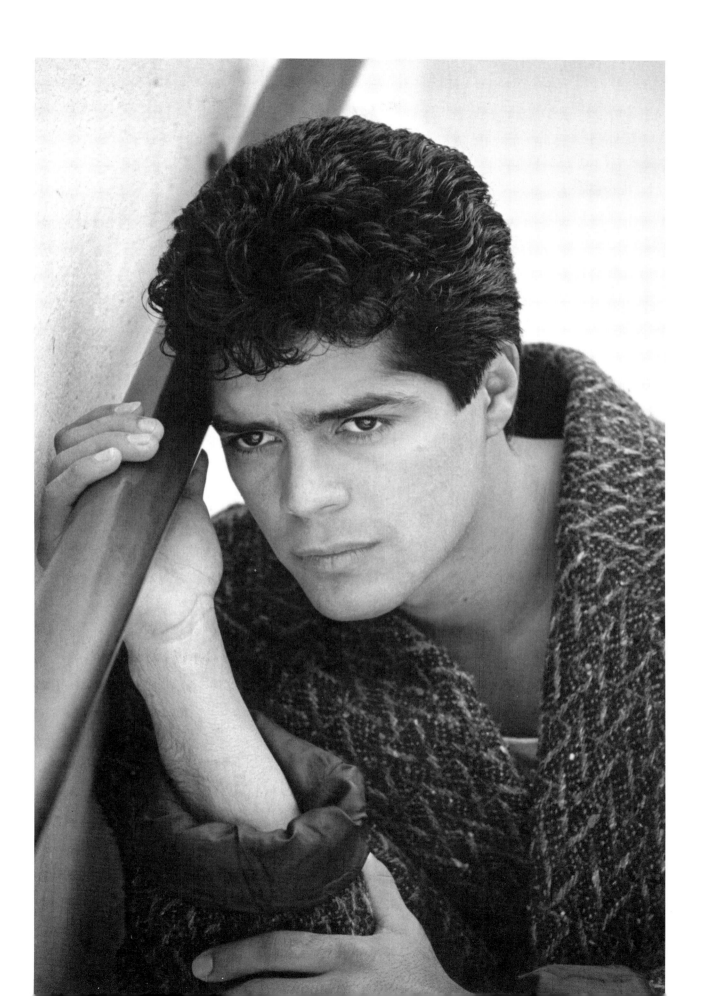

my rebellious teen years, when I wanted as much respect as she did. I didn't understand why, after growing up with the *Brady Bunch*, there was a monopoly on respect in my family. It was just the whole 'Latin thing.'

WHAT WERE YOU LIKE IN HIGH SCHOOL?

I was a very reluctant loner. I had a lot of time to be introspective. I was the Walter Mitty of the South Bronx. I was quite a dreamer and quite a healer. I tried to be the class clown a lot, unlike some of the characters I've portrayed. Before *La Bamba*, I think people perceived me as being a somber, tough street kid with a simple mind and a big heart. I was quite a chance-taker. I remember once my mother went to Puerto Rico to check up on some property she owned there, and I didn't want to.stay in the house alone. I couldn't miss any more school or be late—I had a lateness problem—or they were going to throw me out. So I decided to go to school at two in the morning and camp out there. I snuck over a wall from the parking lot, and I scaled another wall inside the courtyard. I found an open window; and I got in. I was terrified. I thought they had Doberman Pinschers. I ended up falling asleep on the auditorium stage.

WAS THE HIGH SCHOOL FOR PERFORMING ARTS A GOOD TRAINING?

Performing Arts gives kids like me, who are not very disciplined, a structural level. I won't deny I have a degree of talent, but talent without context is like a bullet without a barrel—it's not as effective. I didn't understand, nor did most of the kids, what was meant by "the state of being" or "the character's intentions" or "the rhythm of the scene." You had an idea, but it really didn't mean much. Only afterwards did all this stuff start falling in place. They planted the seeds that I was later to sow. It was a high school made up of marchers of different drummers. I couldn't have sur-

vived in a regular high school; I would have committed suicide. I was already suicidal in Performing Arts.

WHY?

Because of the clique system. I was different. I would say things not everyone wanted to hear, especially girls. Girls just didn't want to hear what I had to say. I was a pain in the ass because I was a very passionate young man. I wanted to be in love, but I never found anyone to reciprocate or felt someone was worthy enough to be in love with me.

DID YOU LOVE YOURSELF THEN?

I don't know. Part of me did and part of me didn't. It's that yin/yang dichotomy that's so strange. Ever since I was five years old, I felt that there was a higher being, watching, hoping and caring for my success. That's what has really stopped me from being a self-destructive person. We all go through so much pain in our lives, and we don't know what it is. Sometimes, when we don't think we can bear it anymore, we'll see someone's life much worse than our own, and then we'll shut up.

WHEN DID YOU DECIDE YOU WANTED TO BE AN ACTOR?

I never decided; it was something that was inevitable. As a five year old, I said I wanted to be a scientist, a lawyer and President of the United States; I believed I could do all of those things very well. I had a connection to them all, an understanding. I realized as an actor I could be all of these things—I could be anything.

WHAT WERE YOUR GOALS WHEN YOUR FIRST STARTED OUT, AND HOW HAVE THEY CHANGED?

I wanted to be rich and famous, lotsa sex. My professional goal was just to become a very popular actor, the best actor I could be, which one day would be the best one around. As I got older, however, I got wiser, and I realized you can't be the "best actor." I figured I'll never get to best-actor

status, except maybe with an Oscar, and that's not a good gauge or authority on actors. I slowly began to realize I wanted people to love me. My goal as an actor today is to make a difference.

ARE YOU GETTING A LOT OF SCRIPTS SUBMITTED TO YOU NOW?

I'm getting a few. I'm not in the place professionally I can—or *should*—be in. All the great stuff goes to Tom Cruise, Rob Lowe and the all-American stars first, and then it will trickle down to me eventually. Therefore, I get a lot of scripts that wouldn't be considered, couldn't get there or have been rejected. I read them, and most of the stories need work. I'm co-producing two, and I have to do an amazing amount of work on both of them. I can't buy a new car right now, so I have to fix-up an old one.

WHAT DO YOU LOOK FOR IN A SCRIPT?

A good story; entertainment. Those are the most important two things, and then comes depth. If it's not a deep story, why should I bother? If it can't fulfill the intellectual and emotional desires of a large range of people, including the sophisticated, why bother? Why just do *Rambo*? That can only satisfy the kids. I feel cheated when I see things like that; I feel like a fool. I'm paying my hard-earned money to see a cartoon of people killing each other. We're exercising this hatred inside of us. Basically, I like taking people on a journey, because I'm a director at heart. One day I will direct feature films. I look for a journey because for six or seven dollars, I think people should go somewhere.

WHEN YOU ACCEPT A ROLE, DO YOU CONSIDER THE EFFECT THE FILM WILL HAVE ON YOUR PEERS?

I'm very conscientious. I don't like being a slave to the world's fickle tastes, though. I won't play a character if he or the story has no redeeming qualities. If the story

insinuates that it's good to kill babies or makes sex the ultimate object of life, I'm not going to do it. I don't want any *Birthdays for Bonzo* because that's not what I'm about. I'm truly concerned with heightening the consciousness of the world.

WHAT HAD BEEN YOUR BIGGEST SACRIFICE FOR SUCCESS?

Privacy. Not that I ever really wanted it, but boy do I want it now. You sacrifice the ability to be left alone if you want to be, and also the ability to know if someone is being completely honest with you. To find someone you can get along with in life is hard enough, but when you're an actor it's even harder. There's always a degree of mistrust that shouldn't be there, but it is anyway.

WHAT'S THE BIGGEST MISCONCEPTION ABOUT YOU?

That I'm superficial. People see me out in public and usually get the wrong impression. I always try to be gracious and giving, but often those actions are misconstrued. Many times, I spread myself too thin and try to communicate with everyone, so people think I'm shallow, and it's far from the truth. I believe you can be a heavyweight and nice to people at the same time.

DO YOU THINK OF YOURSELF AS A TEACHER?

I think of myself as a *student*/teacher. I don't think a teacher is really effective if he ever stops acknowledging he is still a student.

HOW DOES YOUR IMAGE DIFFER FROM YOU AS A PERSON?

I don't know the full extent of my image. I know people think I'm this broody, Latin, sexual god, but I'm a person who thinks and feels a lot. I'm just a human being. I don't think we should limit ourselves to being this or that—we are all so much more. I believe we are all part of each other.

IS BEING AN ACTOR EVER A STRUGGLE FOR YOU?

Yeah. I'm my own biggest critic. I know my potential. If people are wowed now—oh boy, oh boy. I used to think if I were Aryan, people would look at me and say, "He has the makings of a great actor." Because I'm

not, they might say, "He's a great Hispanic actor." It limits me, and that sometimes gets in my way.

WHAT DO YOU LIKE BEST ABOUT SUCCESS?

Success is an abused word. What you, someone else or I think of as success may be three totally different things. For me, growing is success. In this business, all of a sudden you receive carte blanche treatment in certain situations, which means that you can be reckless and abuse it or you can use it in a positive way.

WHAT SPIRITUAL THINGS ARE IMPORTANT TO YOU?

Almost all. A spiritual reality is something most people don't try to attain honestly. What is reality? It's a path you walk on blindfolded. You develop an insight that leads the way. Because you trust in that heartfelt feeling, you take chances. You cannot grow strong without taking risks. The little bird cannot learn how to fly unless it's thrown out of the nest. I think spiritual realities are very important. Reading *The Uranta Book* put a lot into perspective for me. It's the most incredible book of wisdom I've ever come across. I've been exposed to it for about six years now. It has the most objective view of reality I've ever come across. *The Uranta Book* quotes 28 illustrations of high human philosophy. One of them is very special as far as my art is concerned. It says the high mission of any art is, by its illusions, to foreshadow a higher universe—reality—to crystallize the emotions of time into eternity.

IF TWO OTHER ACTORS WERE UP FOR THE SAME PART AS YOU AND EACH HAD IDENTICAL QUALIFICATIONS, WHY SHOULD A DIRECTOR PICK YOU OVER THE OTHER TWO ACTORS?

Because of my motivations; I've developed noble desires. There's an honesty in my work. It's not complete, but it's something I want to develop. I have staying power because of that mission. I won't abandon it.

IS THAT FEELING WHAT KEPT YOU GOING DURING YOUR DRY SPELL BETWEEN *BAD BOYS* AND *LA BAMBA*?

That's not how I got there—it's *why* I got

there. I could have taken a lot of work and been on TV series, but I don't want to sell soap or cars.

HOW DID YOU SURVIVE?

I don't know. Faith had a lot to do with it. Every once in a while, I'd scrape bottom. I remember signing autographs once, and wanting to ask the person for 30¢ to ride the subway. I think those experiences are some of my fondest, though; they make me realize it's not about the superficial things. Life is not about getting on *Entertainment Tonight* or *Lifestyles of the Rich and Famous*. The prize is not the prize itself, but the journey, and realizing what it is that will make life worthwhile for you.

WHAT SOCIAL ISSUES ARE IMPORTANT TO YOU?

Human rights. I cried the other night after seeing a woman who had been burned by Pinochets's soldiers in Chile. We all know soldiers are not the wisest people on the face of this planet. I support anyone who is about freedom of personal expression, and not hatred or oppression.

WHAT DO YOU DO TO MAKE A DIFFERENCE?

I talk to the press and voice my opinions in hope that I will be contacted by groups that have similar opinions as I do. I am trying to keep as conscious as possible without being obsessive. "What we don't know doesn't hurt us" is the attitude in America, and I think that is wrong. We put a little too much trust in the government. It's like wondering why you get cancer after eating TV dinners your whole life. Americans have to start thinking.

HOW DO YOU THINK YOU FIT INTO THE CONTEXT OF *THE NEW BREED*?

There was a new breed in Marlon Brando's day that James Dean was a part of, so I can accept being part of that as opposed to the "brat pack." I don't make outrageous amounts of money for the work I do; that's not what it's about for new-breed actors. I think it's time for all actors to realize what they can *really do*, as opposed to just becoming rich and famous. Those who are already on the path to discovering what that is, I feel, fall into the category of the new breed. It's about making a difference.

Alfre Woodard

If you look deep into Alfre Woodard's eyes, you can see her soul. The rich sense of passion and sensitivity she brings to film, stage and television is simply a magnification of her off screen persona. Whether dealing with social issues like rape on *LA Law* or the liberation of South Africa in real life, Alfre's commitment to her craft, life and a profound sense of right and wrong sets her apart from most people. Her priority is to make a difference.

WHAT WAS YOUR CHILDHOOD LIKE?

I grew up in a small three-bedroom house in Tulsa, Oklahoma. Both my mother and father come from families of 12, and they "went forth and multiplied," so there weren't very many people around I *wasn't* related to. My relatives were over constantly. I remember the sound of laughter and the buzz of a million people trying to be heard. If you wanted to say something, even if you were two or three, you damn well better have figured out a way to jump in there and make it interesting to get everyone's attention. If my parents had been born in another era, they would have been hippies, but they just ended up being great universal people who had strong ties to the land. It was impossible not to be real around them.

I had a fun childhood. The only time I was uncomfortable was when I had to go outside of the house. Being a mixed socioeconomic black community, three blocks away from me were families with dirt floors. My family was well-off, but I was keenly aware when I was young that things were not equal. I was always called the "sensitive" child.

I remember when I was about eight, I walked into the living room one night and burst into tears. My father asked what was wrong. I said, "I just read in *My Weekly Reader* that a hundred people died in a flood in India." My dad said, "Wipe your face—you can't help nobody by cryin'. Do you homework and maybe you can help someone someday."

WHEN DID YOU DECIDE TO BECOME AN ACTRESS?

When I was 15. I was in Catholic school and a sister recruited me into a play. It was an original musical with a lot of Simon & Garfunkel and Led Zeppelin. I remember jumping around in a pink jumpsuit under a strobe light saying things like, "I am here. I have being." I was a big hit, and the nun made me take her two-hour acting class once a week. Once I got into that class, I realized acting was my identity—it was

who I *was*. There were no answers, no right or wrong. Acting to me was complete, absolute, infinite possibility.

SO WHAT DID YOU DO WHEN YOU GRADUATED FROM HIGH SCHOOL?

I went to Boston University. I wanted to get a degree because there was then the mistaken notion that if you didn't have a college degree, you'd drop into a hole that goes to China. I've known since I was a child that I wanted to live my life in Southern California—I'm sure it had something to do with the sunshine and Disneyland at first—so I went to Boston first to experience a different culture.

WHAT WAS YOUR FIRST PROFESSIONAL ROLE?

I was in a play called "Horatio" at the Arena Stage in Washington, D.C. It was a musical, and I'm not a singer or dancer, but I guess I moved well and chanted loudly. I was going to be part of Arena Stage's repertory company, but after so many years of training, eight hours a day followed by three hours of crew plus performing in plays, I knew I had to go to the next level, which is the personalization of the craft. From my orientation of growing up in the Southwest, that meant making movies, so I moved to L.A.

WHAT DID YOU GET OUT OF TRAINING?

I had discipline and a lot of information, but there was a point for me where I had to toss all of that off and try to remember why I wanted to act in the first place, to rediscover the thing that happened to me in drama class at Kelley high school.

DID TRAINING EXTINGUISH THAT SPARK?

I didn't lose that, but my focus was very different. In training, the focus becomes perfecting that spark—it's like building a wonderful bench. The idea, the *need* for that bench, comes first. Then you've got to find the right wood, chop it, sand it, cut it, carve it and do all sorts of things to

make that piece of wood into the perfect bench, all the while staying true to the style you're working in. Sometime in the middle of all that work, you might wake up, look out into the horizon and remember why you wanted to make the bench. That's when you have come up on *your* personal craft. It's a blending of all your training and the natural fire that was there in the first place.

SO DID YOU START MAKING MOVIES AS SOON AS YOU GOT TO LOS ANGELES?

No. It took me about two years. I have a very deep and Africanic look, which most black Americans have. There is a standard of what is considered beautiful and salable in this business and in society, and I completely don't fit into it. I'm where I am today because of perseverance and my belief that good intentions and preparation win out; you have to be patient and let that happen. My first agent didn't send me out *once* in a year and a half. I left him, and no one seemed to know what to do with me until I hooked up with the agent I have now, who I've been with for six years.

It's *hard* to get a job. The easiest thing for an actor to do, if they've done preparation, is act; it's a matter of who can take and last through all of the shit. You've got to deal with the social problems of people you're trying to get a job from, and then you have to consider it is a business. It's like, "How much seasoning do we put into a Frito?" That's how they decide if someone is right for a part. Well, very black girls were just not "in." There are so many incredibly gifted actors who we will never see.

WHY?

They didn't have whatever it took to make it through the maze. If you're an artist, especially an actor, what it takes to get a job is in complete opposition to what makes you a good artist. You're damn lucky if you can figure out and develop the other part. The thing that will help you get

a job is the same thing that would help you win student council president or Miss Congeniality in a beauty contest. I don't think actors generally have that quality, because they've always been on the fringes. Even if they were well-loved and popular, the way I was, they're still on the fringes. You've got to be to have any sense of perspective to bring to your work—you've got to have been observing. You cannot have been in the mainstream and be a good actor. There has had to have been a time in your life when there was a wall there and you were looking in.

AND WAS IT TOUGHER FOR YOU BECAUSE YOU WERE A BLACK WOMAN?

It has not been tough for me at all, but that's because of my sense of reality. I'm no fool—I understand statistics, and an actor's chances of success; you have to be a madman to go into this business. I also understand I am part of a population that is pushed outside of the fruitful part of this society. Everybody says, "Well, I know lots of rich black people," and that may be true, but there are thousands of people we forget about. They're in communities where you don't go, where I don't go unless I know someone and they take me there. So what was my possibility of mounting a life in a nonexistent situation. I really had to know I needed to act; I needed to know I had a story to tell. My reality has always been the only thing standing between me and getting something done is whether I do it or not. I know the history of those who have come before me, but, as in the other parts of my life, I can't accept someone else's reality—and if it's negative, I always assume it doesn't apply to me and it won't manifest in my life. As actors, the only control we really have is over ourselves. So many other people, most of whom do not have the sensitivity, awareness, intelligence and, lord knows, the creativity an actor has, try to hold things over your head. They are the people with the power to hire you.

For the first eight years of my career, I worked once a year for three weeks. Once I didn't work for 15 months. It wasn't like I was sitting around waiting for work, though. I went on with what I would have been doing anyway. If I had focused on not working, I'd be so filled with bitterness and craziness, it would have gotten to my openness. If that was taken away, I wouldn't have had anything. I knew I'd eventually be doing what I wanted, and what you get to do and when you get to do it is very individualized—you can't do something in someone else's time. If you don't get a job, it wasn't your job to begin with, and it's probably for the best you didn't get it because it would have been disastrous if it wasn't really yours.

WHAT WERE YOUR GOALS WHEN YOU FIRST STARTED OUT AND HOW HAVE THEY CHANGED?

When I first started out, I wanted to be a world renowned classical actress who worked at the Open Gate Theater. As I've gotten some of the things I wanted, though, I realize I have less of a personal sense, less need. When you're getting the things you want, a lot of responsibility comes with it. I realize the power of the medium in which I work, and as I've grown and matured as a citizen of the world, I've come to realize my personal freedom is the least important thing when it comes to the statement I'm making. I must be conscious of the statement I'm making.

WHAT DO YOU LOOK FOR IN A SCRIPT?

I don't really look for anything. If I pick up a script, I start to read it silently and I start to develop different voices in my head; if the mechanism trips off automatically, that's what keeps me reading. Within two pages, I usually know if I like something and if it's for me to do. The most important thing is always: Is this a story that needs to be told? The second most important thing is: Do I have anything new to bring to it? If I don't, whether I want to do it or not, I won't. That's like jerking off.

WHAT KIND OF ROLES ARE YOU LOOKING FOR?

I'm open. I think a good writer has a better idea of what good roles are, so I depend on good writers to find me. I want to do projects that assume people are wise, not necessarily educated, but that assume an intelligence. I want to entertain but also provide information.

WHAT SOCIAL ISSUES ARE IMPORTANT TO YOU?

I don't think most Americans understand the power of our government and the havoc they wreak around the world. I see things in my travels that bother me. What used to be the thrust for what is called Americanism is now called "the left"—liberalism. Rather than pushing forward the way we used to be, leading in terms of attracting people to democracy through showing them the good, we beat them with sticks. The group of Americans that are called liberal are now trying to run around the world, sweeping up after this new conservatism that is now called Americanism. Right now, the most important thing going on—not just for me but for the entire world—is the liberation of South Africa.

For the world at large, it's like an addict family problem—it's dirty. For South Africa itself, it's absolutely impossible for it to go into the twenty-first century. It's like Nazi Germany: The architects of apartheid left the Third Reich—that's how it came into being. Because of economics, the Western world has made it very palatable, whereas they couldn't bear it the first time around in Germany.

SO WHAT ARE YOU DOING TO MAKE A DIFFERENCE?

Well, I'll tell you what I'm doing, and I don't know what difference it makes, but it's the only thing I can think of to do. I'm involved with the African National Congress, which is what the largest percentage of South African people, black and white, look to as a foundation for a free South Africa. I try to help raise money, lend a face and be involved with rallies and things. Instead of talking about how I keep cellulite off my thighs in interviews, I talk about South Africa. We have the attention span of children—we forget about things very quickly, and forget things that go on every day. People in power depend on our forgetfulness to do what they do. I try to talk as much as possible, wherever I am, about South Africa. If people are talking about it, we won't forget it.

HOW DO YOU FEEL YOU FIT INTO THE CONTEXT OF THE NEW BREED?

I think there have always been people like myself around who are actors, but it's like there are cameras constantly panning the room. Maybe the camera hasn't been on people like me. Maybe now it's our time.

Rick Rossovich

Rick Rossovich's father had a dream. He wanted to take his family away from the hassles and pressures of urban America and bring them up in a rural environment. A combination of good investments and smart planning allowed him to realize his dream, and when Rick was 10, the senior Rossovich moved his family to a ranch near Lake Tahoe in Northern California.

Though it wasn't *Days of Heaven*, living on 200 acres of land with cows, pigs and horses came with an entirely different set of responsibilities than Rick had experienced in the city. He wanted a minibike, but instead he'd have to spend his free time milking cows or feeding pigs. The nearest neighbor was miles away, so in the summer he wouldn't see much of his friends, but then there were chores to keep him occupied.

It was hard, but Rick feels it taught him responsibility and discipline. It gave him a sense of commitment which continues to have a profound impact on his life and work as an actor. It is this commitment to craft that has kept him working steadily for 10 years.

Although most of his parts have been character roles, his work in *Roxanne* as Daryl Hannah's bumbling love interest has opened up the possibility of Rick playing romantic leading men, an idea he finds amusing yet bewildering. Between films, he spends his time at home in the Hollywood Hills, fixing up the large Mediterranean-style house where he lives with his wife Eva and their son Roy. Rick's priority today is to try to find a balance between his responsibility to his family and his commitment to his craft.

HOW WOULD YOUR MOTHER DESCRIBE YOU AS KID?

My mother would probably say I was a sensitive kid. I was always in and out of love as a teenager. I would never break up with my girlfriends. I'd always make it horrible enough so that they would have to leave me. I had a big mouth in high school, but I did it to make everyone laugh. I hung out with everybody—the guys who smoked pot, the jocks and the brains.

WHAT ATHLETICS DID YOU DO?

I was a high school all-American football player. My brother played professional football, so I had all that pressure to live up to.

DID YOUR FATHER WANT YOU TO PLAY FOOTBALL TOO?

No, my parents never pressured me to do anything. They loved the fact that I got started in an art career in my early teens.

WHAT WERE YOUR GOALS AS AN ACTOR WHEN YOU FIRST STARTED OUT AND HOW HAVE THEY CHANGED?

When you first start out, you grab at anything. My first job was in a little non-union picture, and I was thrilled. Of course, everyone wants to star in *Raging Bull* or as Stanley in *Streetcar Named Desire*, but you have to start somewhere. It was a Korean karate film. I knew a guy who was costuming the picture; he told me they were looking for someone to play a secret CIA agent. I went up to the office on Sunset Blvd. on the tenth floor. It was all new to me. I saw some guy in the outer office with some makeup on and I thought, "Wow, man, this is wild!" I went in and bluffed my way through the whole thing. I got the job, did three days work and got paid 90 bucks. I did stunts, I did lines and I got kicked all over the place. I figured, "Oh, this isn't so hard." The next job I got was as a stand-in for an actor—I stood in for four and a half months for lighting. That was good for me, because I

got to see what a cinematographer does, what the prop guys do, what the grips do—I got to learn about the business on a whole different level.

AT THAT POINT DID YOU WANT TO BE AN ACTOR?

Yeah, more than anything. I figured, "God, it all rides on one guy's shoulders. Everyone works for an hour or two to get everything set up, and then it's all focused on the actor. If it doesn't work, then there are 65 or a hundred people standing around watching this guy fuck up, and he'd better get it together—he'd better catch the ball."

I like that kind of pressure, because sometimes it can spur on something that's not expected. It's your form—everything is focused on you. You can do it, you can change it. A lot of people complain that in film acting you are not as in control as you are on a theater stage. I say bullshit—I'm in control when the camera rolls; I pull all kinds of shit they never expect.

LIKE WHAT?

To do stuff in scenes—grab something, hit a prop that you never told anyone about, say a line that nobody's expecting to hear—just make it happen when the camera rolls. I love it.

WHAT DO YOU LIKE BEST ABOUT BEING AN ACTOR?

The freedom of it the freedom of the work and the freedom when you're *not* working. It's a lot of pressure, but it's a free career—it's always going to change, it's always going to be different. When I came to Hollywood, I was 17. My brother was down here, and he had just retired from his football career and was getting started in stunt work. I wanted to move out then. But everyone said "You're too young; go back and get an education first." So I did. I studied art history and sculpture. I had this whole studio on this ranch where I used to go out and tear stone apart with a pneumatic hammer. There was dust everywhere. I was kind of prolific—I turned out a lot of sculpture and I *sold* a lot of it.

WHY DIDN'T YOU PURSUE A CAREER AS AN ARTIST?

It wasn't fast enough—there was no immediate gratification.

IS THAT WHAT ACTING IS FOR YOU?

Sometimes. It's that and the risk of falling on your face at the same time. There's just as big a chance for failure as there is for success in this business. It's kind of exciting to tread that edge, that cliff. You can always fall—I've fallen lots of times.

WHAT DO YOU DO WHEN YOU FALL?

I pick myself up. You always have another chance. Look at some of the shit some of these actors turn out—the embarrassment they survive—and they keep working. Who knows why people continue to want to see them? I hope it never gets that bad for me.

WHAT WAS YOUR NEXT JOB, AFTER THE STAND-IN JOB?

I studied for about three years, and I started to get little roles here and there. When you're starting out, you jump at a stupid guest spot on something like *BJ and the Bear*, because you want to get a foothold. I mean, you can walk into town and all of a sudden you're in *The Breakfast Club* . . . well, whoopdee-fucking-do—

lucky you! But where do you go from *there*? You might sit on your ass for five years waiting for another role to come along. I started out gradually, and I started at the very bottom—a non-union picture, a stand-in position, a shit TV series. It was good for me, because I didn't expect to be in a big movie right off the bat. I knew I could start slow and learn at my own pace, and here I am almost 10 years later—I had the chance to find my own way and not be pushed before I was ready.

HOW DO YOU FEEL ABOUT HOLLYWOOD?

This town is full of people who want to stop you—who try to put walls in your way to keep you from moving forward. You have to be strong in yourself; you have to create your own possibilities.

HOW HAVE YOU DONE THAT?

My first real break in film was in *Lords of Discipline*. I was with a small agency at the time, and I had just gotten in there by the skin of my teeth. I read the script in my acting class, and I knew I could play this role to a tee—it had all the elements I related to. The character was the most powerful guy on campus. He was crazy, and still like a little child. I worked on the script for six months before I had a chance—or could *create* the chance—to read for the film. I told my agents they had to get me a meeting on this film, and they said, "You're not ready for it yet. What have you done, "*BJ and the Bear*"? You want to do a big movie for Paramount? Are you kidding?" They wouldn't get me the meeting. I went to Paramount myself—I made my *own* opportunity. I went into the director's office; he asked me how I saw the character. It was the most important meeting of my career, but I was so relaxed. I knew the character so well; I had worked on it so much. I knew he had to hire me, because I could bring the part to life. I told him I thought that Dante Pignetti, "the Pig," had a strong sense of family, and that his mother was really important to him. The director asked me if I really thought so, and I said, "Frank, I want you to meet my mother." She was sitting in the outer office because by chance she was in town and I had brought her to the meeting. When the director met my mom, it was too much for him. It blew him away and I got the job.

But there's always someone there to

say no. The executives loved me, but they said I wasn't big enough. When they asked me how much I weighted, I told them 200 pounds. They said, "Listen, we have ten weeks before we start principal photography; we want you to gain 25 pounds, and we'll put it into your contract that you have to weigh 225 pounds, and we're going to weigh you when you get to London." Well, I had lied—I weighed about 187 pounds. So it was another roadblock, but I was committed, and I gained 35 pounds in ten weeks.

THAT'S GREAT.

But then I came back, and all of a sudden my agents said, "Well, he's a big lunk. Gee, OK, now we can put him in the big-lunk category." That's the thing about Hollywood—they try to categorize you. I had to get away from that, and it wasn't easy, but then I got a role as a skinny guy, and then it was OK again.

DO YOU EVER GET ANGRY?

Yeah, sure—angry and pissed off. I break things; I get crazy—I don't let a lot of people know that, though. I lead a very private life—I don't have very many friends; I have a lot of acquaintances. I'm kind of sad about that sometimes. I wish I had more friends; I think I'd be a better person if I did. It's gotten to the point where, when I do meet new people, they don't tell me anything about themselves—they just want to know about me. It's always the same question, or the same repetition of questions, and it's boring—it bores me to death. That's why I've chilled away from that.

DO YOU FEEL YOU'VE HAD TO COMPROMISE YOUR VALUES IN THE ROLES YOU'VE CHOSEN?

If anyone says they've never compromised their values, they're lying—everyone compromises to a certain extent. I always want to do "A" work, but now I have more flexibility than I used to.

DID YOU TURN DOWN A TELEVISION SERIES FOR A LOT OF MONEY AFTER ROXANNE?

I could have done a television series, but I knew it would be a dead end. They offered me a lot of money, but big deal—it wasn't going to make me happy; I don't need much more than I already have. I could have done another film for twice the

money as *Secret Ingredient*, a film I did in Yugoslavia, but the role wasn't as good. That role allowed me to play three characters in one film—I might not have that chance again ever. I feel if I can have an opportunity like *Lords of Discipline, Roxanne* or *Secret Ingredient* every few years, than I'm ahead of the game.

WHAT KIND OF ROLES ARE YOU LOOKING FOR NOW?

I look for roles I can play on a lot of different levels. *Secret Ingredient* may never be seen in this country, but it made me jump personal levels, as an actor and as a human being, and I'll be stronger for it in the next role I do. That's what it's all about—getting stronger.

WHAT DOES GETTING STRONGER MEAN TO YOU?

Knowing myself better, knowing what my limitations are and learning how to get around them—so that, ultimately they're no longer limitations.

DO YOU CONSIDER WHAT EFFECT THE ROLES YOU CHOOSE WILL HAVE ON PEOPLE?

I vacillate on that; it changes from film to film. Now, if Willem [Dafoe] goes off to do this film about Christ with Martin Scorsese, then that's on a whole different level than *Streets of Fire*. You have to build up to a point where you can choose stronger projects.

HOW DO YOU APPROACH A ROLE?

I try to compile a history of my character and see what he's gone through and what he has to look forward to, and how that affects the situation he's in in the piece. I think you have to be honest as an actor—you have to pull out a part of yourself and use that as a basis to make the character real. It's important, though, to keep your life in balance. After all, we're human beings—we have lives besides what we're doing on the screen. I have a family, I have a wife, I have a house, I have my commitments and responsibilities—and if I let all that go while I'm working, what happens when I'm done? A project only lasts a few months.

SO YOU NEVER LET GO COMPLETELY?

Yeah, I do—100%. I let go in Yugoslavia, and I almost lost my whole life! That's why

I'm saying what I'm saying right now; there's such a delicate line. I came home and I wasn't ready to come home, so I brought *hell* home with me. It was hard.

Stephen Baldwin

WHAT HAPPENED IN YUGOSLAVIA? WHAT WAS THE EXPERIENCE LIKE?

I'm of Yugoslavian heritage, so it was a real experience to go back where my ancestors came from. Everybody treated me like a golden child, because I was in some phenomenal film called *Top Gun*. Right. They didn't remember which character I played so much as the fact that I was in it. The real thing that was there for me, however, was the role, and the chance for me to get up and go to work every morning and have a real challenge. That was from day one until we finished. I had to speak Serbo-Croatian; I had to do mime; I had to work when I fell down some steps and nearly broke my ankle. It was all a fight, but it was all for love too—because I really loved the project.

WOULD YOU CONSIDER DOING A NUDE SCENE?

I don't care about taking my clothes off. I think most directors have enough taste that they're going to keep the material on a certain level of decency, so that it can be seen by a majority of people. Your body's your body—it's one of your tools, and you have to use it accordingly.

IF TWO OTHER ACTORS WERE UP FOR THE SAME PART AS YOU AND ALL THREE OF YOU WERE EQUAL IN TERMS OF LOOKS, TALENT, EXPERIENCE, ETC., WHY SHOULD A DIRECTOR CHOOSE YOU OVER THE OTHER TWO ACTORS?

Because I'm committed; because I have a lot more heart. In *Lords of Discipline*, we did a scene on a 16-inch window ledge four stories up. There were no wires, no safety net, no boxes, no nothing beneath me—we're talking 60 feet to the ground. I was screaming at 200 cadets on the battalion courtyard, a two-page monologue where I'm screaming my guts out, running back and forth on this 16-inch ledge. I never quit. They had a wire rigged up for me, but it was impeding my performance, so I made them take it away—it made the scene more real. I'm completely committed. When a camera roles, I'm there. I never quit. Never.

I have three brothers—Alec, Daniel and Billy. I'm the youngest. We grew up in Massapequa, Long Island, outside of New York City. Whenever my brothers would get mad at me, I would run under my mother's skirt for protection. She would always stand up for me; I was her baby. My father was a social studies teacher; he taught high school for 30 years. He was a great man, a selfless, compassionate man whose life was dedicated to teaching and being there for all of his students.

I didn't fully appreciate his greatness until after his death; He instilled in my brothers and me a sense of responsibility toward society. If I were ever to create a film project, I would like to base it on my father's life.

As a kid, I was a little terror, but I was also able to charm, and I loved to entertain. In high school, I was the cutup and a ham, but I knew how to pull the wool over people's eyes and get away with murder. I'd have friends stand guard while I was behind the wall kissing some girl I wasn't supposed to, and I'd try to just generally get away with as much insanity as I possibly could.

It was in high school that I first started acting, and I found the more I pursued it, the more I became interested in it. When I touched on human emotion and how I could put myself in a situation, it just fascinated me. There has been nothing in my life so far that has even come close.

On my first day of class at the American Academy of Dramatic Arts in New York city, my teacher asked the class if anyone was there to study acting because they wanted to become famous; eight people raised their hands. Then he asked if anyone was there to study acting because they wanted to become rich; ten people raised their hands. Finally, he asked if anyone was there to study acting but they didn't know why; me and another guy raised our hands. He said, "you two stay; the rest of you leave until tomorrow—you don't need to be part of this discussion." And he wasn't kidding.

We became his first friends in that class, because we were there for the most instinctual reasons, and we spent the morning talking about acting and instinct. I told him I had started acting because I felt I had a spark, a niche that let me understand human emotion more than the next guy, and I wanted to explore that.

Acting is simple, but not many people have a clue of what's involved spiritually, emotionally, creatively or energy-wise. You have to put yourself in a situation, make it real as life in that moment—either basing it on your own life experience or creating it with your imagination. Whenever I pick up a piece of paper that is commercial copy, TV copy, film copy or stage copy, the techniques may alter, but the essence of what the life of the emotion is—or what rationally creates it or makes anyone believe it—that never changes.

I'm looking for projects that are going to freak me out, and really, really attract me on an instinctual level from the second I lay eyes on them. *Motherland*, a film I did last year, was like that—it excited me from the moment I read it. The film dealt with the Soviet invasion of Afghanistan, which is one of the biggest hypocrisies going on in the world right now. I was in this explosive situation, but what I really had to deal with was a sensitive individual—this Russian kid was in a music class somewhere in Stalingrad one day, and *poof*, overnight he was in Afghanistan with maybe two weeks to train. I had to live, feel and breathe in the reality of his situation, and make it seem real.

I had never even had a passport before going to Israel to do that movie. Before I left, I was told I was going to receive military training, and at the time it sounded really cool. But when I got there and I was in the middle of the training, I remember thinking, "What am I doing here?" I was scared, frightened, and all of a sudden, I felt an intense affinity for my character.

I remember sitting on top of the tanks we were training with at 2:00 A.M. and looking at the stars—there are a million stars over Israel. I sat there listening to Mozart on my Walkman, trying to get the whole spiritual vibe from that land, and at that moment, on a moralistic spiritual level, it made me want to pursue acting even more. I realized, "man, there's no way, unless I'm reincarnated into a Soviet boy, that I'm ever going to live something like this." It was really a trip.

There are only a few people in my life who really have a grip on what I'm trying to accomplish as an actor, who know my level of intensity—and that's because I've let them in. Acting is a never-ending struggle for me because of my outrageous pursuit of perfection; it's almost on a psychotic level.

It's an energy I feel. When I want a part really badly, I freak out sometimes. When I go into an audition, I can't be so into a script that the director will think I'm a fucking weirdo, so I try to control that. The fire in my eyes, so to speak, will get the point across to him.

That happened when I got "Out In America," this play I did off-Broadway with Daryl Hannah. I got the part from a basic standard audition that was on the New York breakdowns. I knew I had to play this character—he was the most passionate human being I've ever come across in a script. He was a pseudo-bisexual. His sister had committed suicide a year earlier, and he was approached in an affectionate way by a friend of his who happened to be a guy.

I didn't have a grip on the sexuality as far as the homosexuality went, until Daryl and I were blocking the big kissing scene, and she tells my character he's sexy, sexy like a girl, and soft and scared like a little boy. By frustrating me and making me angry, she touched on some personal things that unraveled the connection between my sister's death and my sexuality, and not only do I fall in love with her, but I fully understand why I fall in love with her, and how being so vulnerable at a certain moment made me also fall in love with my friend that was a guy. That is what acting is to me, man—it's called *life*.

A gentleman came up to me after the play one night and said, "You know, I watched your work, and the writing was not that good, but I saw everything you were trying to do. You've got this intensity that is far greater than anyone I've ever seen, and I understood your position in the story and I want to thank you for that." That was worth more money than anyone could offer me, man, because that's totally what I want to do. He was living it with me, and that's all I want.

In acting school, we read this book by Edgar Lee Masters called *The Spoon River Anthology*. In one of the monologues, it basically states, "Live your life, man," and that's what I try to do in my work and my life. No matter who says what, what you do or what repercussions there are, if I feel it's right, I live it and go on.

There are a lot of politics involved in this business and a lot of shmoozing that people feel they have to do in order to get somewhere. I personally would rather just bury my head in the ground. What I've done is surround myself with a manager, Pat Reeves, and an agent, Michael Kingman, who support me, fight to get me auditions and keep me in line when I get too crazy; I'm lucky to have that support in my life.

My goal as an actor is to follow my instincts, to tune into that fire raging inside of me. I pursue it in hope that my honesty and conviction will get my point across to my audience.

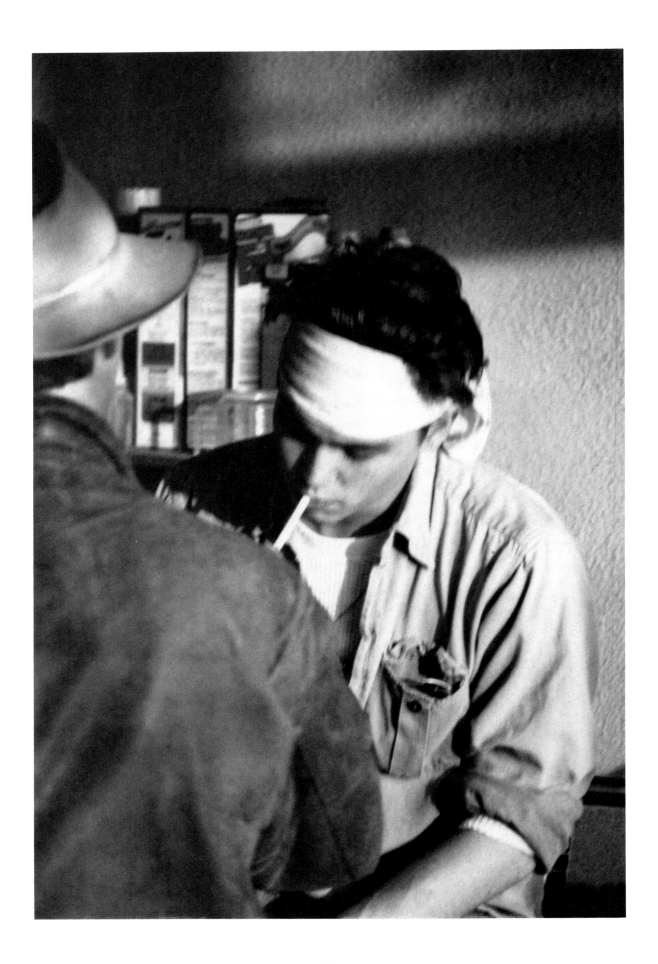

"The first day the actors I cast in PERMANENT RECORD showed up on the set, they were completely different from the people I had met during the audition process— they had probed, researched, and understood the attitudes, backgrounds, and nuances of their characters. They were not Jennifer or Keanu; they were completely committed to character. This commitment will allow them to continue to expand and grow."— **Marisa Silver, Director of PERMANENT RECORD**

Melanie Griffith

Melanie Griffith was a casualty of the Hollywood machine. The victim of a little success and a lot of alcohol, drugs, fast living and insecurity, she forgot where make-believe ended and real life began. Melanie didn't take herself seriously, and as a result, neither did anyone else.

Fate intervened, however, when Melanie was 23. She had been drinking at LeDome, a trendy L.A. restaurant, and was intoxicated as usual. As she stepped into the crosswalk to make her way across Sunset Boulevard, she was struck by a car. Not only did the accident sober her up, it was the catalyst that caused Melanie to begin taking control of her life and career. After recovering, she moved to New York City to study acting with Stella Adler.

Studying radically changed her perspective on acting and being an actress. She says it taught her that giving and making people feel is far more important than anything else. Melanie is no longer the ditsy blonde, playing herself role after role, onscreen and off. Still offbeat and sometimes wacky, she is a complex individual who continuously reveals different sides of herself when you least expect it.

WHAT WAS THE HOUSE LIKE YOU GREW UP IN?

I grew up in an upside-down house overlooking the San Fernando Valley. It was really isolated because there was a lot of foliage—greenery, trees, ivy—and a lot of land. It was kind of like living in a tree-house-style ranch. We had lions and tigers there for about five years, so it was like living in a zoo.

WHY DID YOU HAVE LIONS AND

TIGERS IN SOUTHERN CALIFORNIA?

My mother made this movie in Africa when I was about 12, and she was really taken with the plight of the animals. My stepfather wrote a screenplay about lions, tigers and all kinds of cats, and I got my first lion when I was 13. He lived with me in my bedroom and slept with me at night—he was my best friend. We got more animals, but we couldn't keep them in the end because one of our neighbors complained that one of our lions tried to eat her grandchild. That never really happened—she was just wacko.

HOW WOULD YOUR MOTHER DESCRIBE YOU AS A LITTLE KID?

Her angel—then I grew up. I pretty much left home when I was 14, and that must have been hard for her.

YOU MOVED OUT WHEN YOU WERE 14?

That's when I met Don Johnson. I didn't really move out until I was 15½, but I spent the weekend with him a lot. He used to call me "Pinky." My face looked really young, but my body was developed. I acted really silly. I was so goo-goo-eyed over him. Don was my best friend. I went to Catholic school, but I wasn't Catholic. I had some girlfriends, but no one from whom I was inseparable. By the time I graduated high school when I was 16, I had been around the world.

WHEN DID YOU DECIDE TO BECOME AN ACTRESS?

Well, for a long time, I didn't want to be an actress. When I was 16, I was modeling to make money. We're talking junior modeling, not *Vogue*. Karen Lamm, an actress friend of mine, went up for a film called *Night Moves*. She met Arthur Penn [the film's director], but she wasn't right for the role, so she recommended me. One day, I got this message on my service, and I thought it was a modeling interview. When I got there, I found out it was an acting job, and I told them I didn't want to be an actress. I met with Arthur Penn anyway, and he asked me to work on the script just for the hell of it. Don and I went over it, and I got the part and ended up doing it for the money.

BUT WHEN DID *YOU* DECIDE YOU WANTED TO BECOME AN ACTRESS?

When I was 23, after my accident. Up until that point I had worked a lot, and I thought I was really cool. I started to believe my own press, which is something a lot of people in this town and business go through; it wasn't about what it's about for me now. I didn't have any sort of

technique. I didn't really take it seriously—every character I played was just me. All I did was learn the lines.

WHAT CHARACTERS WERE THOSE?

Nymphettes. I just got too caught up in the Hollywood rat race. I started to drink and do drugs. I didn't take care of myself. After the accident, I went to New York to study with Stella Adler. That was a humbling experience, because nobody gives a shit who you are there. You have to work and you have to be committed; otherwise, you're not taken seriously. Being onstage is completely different from making a movie. It was a wonderful time—it was a time of Campbell's Soup, knishes, the subway and hard work. It made me appreciate what I do.

WHAT DID YOU LEARN AND WHAT DID IT MAKE YOU APPRECIATE?

If you are in the position to make somebody feel something, that's a big responsibility. If you're faking it, you're not being fair to the audience. I learned to open my heart, take chances and be someone else. I discovered acting is what I really want to do, and I wanted to do it for the acting, not for the glory—because there really isn't any glory.

WHAT ARE YOUR GOALS AT THAT POINT AND HOW HAVE THEY CHANGED?

My goal then was to resurrect my career. I had a terrible reputation in the business, and for good reason. I was irresponsible and flaky, and people don't have time for that. Now I want to be a great actress and to give—maybe make someone *feel* something. I want to give the characters I play a realness, so people can relate to them.

WHAT DO YOU LOOK FOR IN A SCRIPT?

Some kind of message, some kind of through-line where the character achieves something that was unachievable or maybe something people around her thought she couldn't do.

WHY ARE THERE NO LEADING LADIES IN HOLLYWOOD TODAY?

Well, there aren't very many good scripts, and most of the good ones are about men. It's also not the studio system anymore. Those actresses were all groomed and nurtured and had publicity people

constantly putting their names out there, making them into what they were. Now it's an individual thing—it's whatever you do with your career and your life and how you deal with things. It must have been more glamorous then to be a movie star. I don't think people have the heroes they did then.

SO BEING AN ACTRESS IS NOT GLAMOROUS?

No way. I work my butt off.

WHAT'S THE BIGGEST MISCONCEPTION ABOUT YOU?

That I'm a sexpot. I took pictures for a magazine the other day, and the photographer wanted me to wear lingerie, to be sexy and to show cleavage. I said, "Look in my eyes. Sexiness can come from there, too." You don't have to use your flesh to be sexy.

ARE NUDE SCENES DIFFICULT FOR YOU?

Yeah.—God, they're difficult! If you don't request a closed set and only the director, the cameraman and those people who absolutely have to be there, it seems like everyone in the *state* shows up! It's amazing the people who crawl out of the woodwork once there's a nude scene. It's not easy. I would never do gratuitous nudity, where I was a bimbo lying on a couch to decorate a set. My nude scene in *Something Wild* took three days to shoot. Jeff [Daniels] and I had just met and it was on the second day of shooting. It was good because it wouldn't have been as awkward if we had shot that scene later on.

HOW DO YOU DIFFER FROM YOUR ON SCREEN IMAGE?

I stay at home with my kid; I go to the market; I read books all the time; I work out. I don't live a fast life. When you're an actor, the roles you choose are the karma you go through in your life. Usually, people have a profession where there's a beginning, a middle and an end; as an actor, you have a beginning, middle and end with every role you do. It seems like the parts that come to you when you have a true heart with your work tie into things you need to work out in your life.

For me, *Body Double* was kind of exorcising the sexpot thing. Not that that was what the story was about, but for me to be that bold, that naked, that ditsy and give my character a heart of gold . . . and there was something really there—it had to be more than what was superficially there. In *Something Wild*, being a wild woman who goes through a metamorphosis of what she really wants made me think about what I really wanted, and whether I have the courage to stand up for what I want. *Working Girl* takes that question one step further.

SO HOW DO YOU APPROACH AND PREPARE FOR A ROLE?

I read the script over and over, and I think about my character and her life before the script begins. Harry Mater Georges, a guy I studied with, says, "Acting is a child's game played with adult rules." If you say to a kid, "Be a policeman," he will become a policeman in a second. Tell the same thing to an adult, and he will try to figure out his motivation and feel—he will have to work as a policeman in order to know what it really feels like. I'm like a child—I use my imagination. I believe in what I'm doing, believe I'm the character I'm playing, take in as much information as I possibly can—and then I let it all go.

WAS FINDING THE RIGHT MANAGER OR AGENT DIFFICULT FOR YOU?

I think I was with every agency in town, and no one believed in me. One of them, the agency I was with when I did *Body Double*, wouldn't even send me up on it. Brian [DePalma] called me up to ask me to introduce him to Jamie Lee Curtis. We all had dinner, but Jamie wasn't interested. I asked Brian, "What about me?" He said, "Stephen [Bauer, her ex-husband] would never let you do it." I said, "Yes he would," and I tested for it and got it. The agency that wouldn't even send me up for the part still wanted their commission; I fired them after that. They didn't believe in me and didn't believe I was ever going to make it. I've been with Triad for three years now, and they're great. Phyllis Carlisle is my manager, and she's great. She's got incredible vision and helps you create a career to keep you working all the time, not to be a humungous movie star.

HAVE YOU CREATED A LOT OF YOUR WORK THROUGH PEOPLE YOU KNOW?

No. I was nine months pregnant when Jonathan [Demme] called me up and asked me to read the *Something Wild* script. I was so flattered that he didn't want anyone else but me for the part.

WHAT HAS BEEN YOUR BIGGEST SACRIFICE FOR SUCCESS?

I've sacrificed a lasting relationship. It's a hard business, and the two times I've been married, it's been to actors and it's been difficult. I don't think it has to be, but somehow, that's the way it's been. I'd like to have a relationship where the guy I meet is my best friend, partner, lover, and it lasts.

IS BEING AN ACTRESS A STRUGGLE FOR YOU?

It's a constant struggle. The whole star trip, and not wanting it but having to deal with it because you want to work, is a struggle. Where do you place your goals? How big do you want to be? You have to find a balance. I don't think you can calculate this business at all, though. It just sort of happens when it's supposed to happen.

IS IT EASY TO GET SUCKED INTO THE MACHINE?

When you're younger it is. It's all ripe for the picking. You get stroked on the back, get a lot of attention and accolades, and it takes a while to get in touch with who you really are. This town doesn't really allow you to do that until you really decide that's what you want.

WHERE DO ALCOHOL AND DRUG ABUSE FALL INTO THE WHOLE SCENE?

I don't know. I wonder if it's as big a problem everywhere as it is in Hollywood. I didn't think alcohol or drugs were ever going to be a problem—everyone else was doing them, too. Everyone was snorting coke and drinking. One day I felt I had to have some, and then it was a problem.

If you get through it and you're strong, you should be here. I like myself now; I didn't like myself then. On drugs, you're not straight and you're not who you really are. It's really painful to get straight and really *find out* who you are. Until you really get the courage to do it, it seems a lot harder than it actually is.

WHAT IS YOUR BIGGEST DISAPPOINTMENT UP TO THIS POINT?

My biggest disappointment is taking a long time to grow up. I don't know if I'll ever grow up, though—I think I have a

different interpretation of what that means. But having a kid has caused me to look at things differently. I have a lot more patience. I am no longer the most important thing—my kid is. I think it's important for actors to have kids because most actors are so fucking egotistical and self-involved. When you have a child that changes.

WHAT SPIRITUAL THINGS ARE IMPORTANT TO YOU?

God is important; I think you have to believe in a higher power. There's someone responsible for all of this. I have a guru—Gurumayi is her name. It wasn't until I met her that my life started to get better and to work. I've done two meditation intensives with her. On the first one, I felt as if I was purged of all the things I dislike about myself—I just let them go. You can do that on your own, but she really helped me. I did another intensive when I was seven months pregnant [with son Alexander]. When Gurumayi felt my stomach, Alexander turned over. Now, when I play a tape of Gurumayi or Muktunanda, Alexander gets so centered. It's nice to be spiritual—it makes you a lot nicer and a lot calmer.

ARE ANY SOCIAL CONCERNS IMPORTANT TO YOU?

You mean like toxic waste, who's going to be the next president, who's *really* going to be the next president? Yeah, I've been involved for about two years with Network—Tom Hayden and Jane Fonda's group. The way our country is being run really scares me. I want to learn more now that I have a child. It's not about human beings anymore—it's about big business.

SO WHAT ARE YOU DOING TO MAKE A DIFFERENCE?

I'm gathering as much information as I can right now to figure out who and what makes sense for me to support. I've been involved with issues like toxic waste, and I've gone to rallies to help raise consciousness in cleaning up the environment.

HOW DO YOU FEEL YOU FIT INTO THE CONTEXT OF THE NEW BREED?

I do what I do to make a difference. I may be offbeat, but I'm not some kind of manufactured person. I'm a survivor. I'm the real thing.

D.B. Sweeney

D. B. Sweeney started acting on a dare. The total jock in high school (soccer in the fall, basketball in the winter, baseball in the spring), D. B.—or "the ween," as he was known to his buddies—was the class clown. He enjoyed humiliating his teachers. After convincing an English professor to change the correct spelling of a fraternity to an incorrect spelling on the blackboard, and then rousing his class into a fit of laughter, the teacher retaliated by challenging the "the ween" to participate in the fall production of the school play.

D. B. accepted the challenge and was surprised to find that acting was a lot like sports, but with one key difference. In sports, he always wanted to be up at the plate in crucial moments—he felt he could get the job done better than the next guy. With acting, however, he could *always* be the key player. Although a motorcycle accident destroyed his dream of becoming a professional baseball player, after graduating from NYU's theater program, D. B. got to live out his baseball player fantasy in John Sayle's *Eight Men Out*, co-starring John Cusack and Charlie Sheen. D. B. also has aspirations of becoming a director; and recently directed "The Shaper" a play he optioned about two aging surfers.

WHAT WAS YOUR EXPERIENCE LIKE STUDYING AT NYU?

It was OK. NYU is sort of a playground for rich kids in a way. Most of the students there would rather be bumming around Europe, but if they quit school, their parents would cut them off. I was cooking at a restaurant, driving a cab, going to school and doing plays. Eventually I felt it was foolish to work so hard for this school. My last year I was on independent study, producing and directing plays in order to get prime parts. I ended up getting a degree from NYU basically by *buying* it. I ran into David Mamet there, and he started a summer theater in Vermont. I was a David Mamet fanatic at the time; at 21, you look for heroes and people to believe in, and his plays seemed like they cut through the bullshit. I participated in his summer theater workshop, out of which the Atlantic Theater Company was born. It didn't feel right for me to continue with them, though. There was too much energy put into talking about the organization and its ideals. I'd been working in a hot kitchen for $50 a night and I didn't have time to talk shop—I just wanted to do plays.

WHAT WERE YOUR GOALS AS AN ACTOR WHEN YOU FIRST STARTED OUT, AND HOW HAVE THEY CHANGED?

They're pretty much the same. I wanted to stay away from doing projects that were full of shit, just for money or stardom. My first job was "The Caine Mutiny Court Martial" on Broadway. There I was an actor, working on Broadway with some really good actors, and I thought that's about as good as it can get. I want to do work that I feel good about because of the work—not where it will get me. What's changed for me lately is that I can actually have some input into making my goals

come true. It used to be a crapshoot—I had to hope someone would hire me.

WHAT KIND OF ROLES ARE YOU LOOKING FOR?

I want to do a lot of different kinds of stuff. It's tricky right now, because people perceive me as the "good son." The same people who make lame decisions about scripts have a limited vision about how they see actors. If you do something successful once, they figure they can count on that forever, and that becomes one of the production elements—they build you into their package. You have to fight against that all the time. I want to continue to explore what I can do. I'm still learning; I'm still discovering my limitations and my possibilities. I read scripts in terms of how they appeal to my sense of challenge.

IS STUDYING IMPORTANT FOR YOUR GROWTH AS AN ACTOR?

I've tried a couple different classes since I started working, and it's strange—as a struggling actor, there's a camaraderie. Once you start working, you leave that group and become a part of another group. That other group is mostly on the West Coast [D.B. lives in N.Y.C.], but I don't feel comfortable with them. I feel like I'm in a place in the middle. I have a lot of non-actor friends I hang out with. I haven't found many working actors who are able to put aside their work and go back into the process of working in a class. I personally hope to find a theater company or a class in which people have a commitment to each other—in which I can grow and find support.

WOULD YOU DO A NUDE SCENE?

I don't know. There are a couple of directors that I would have trouble saying no to about anything—Bernardo Bertolucci and David Lynch. I think I would go with them a long way.

DO YOU CONSIDER WHAT EFFECT A FILM IS GOING TO HAVE ON YOUR PEERS WHEN TAKING A ROLE?

Yeah, I do. In *Garden of Stone*, my character smoked a lot of Camels in the script. Since he was a qualified hero, I didn't want him to smoke. I don't want to add to the idea that movies perpetuate the myth that smoking is cool. I also didn't want people to look up to my character be-

cause of his right-wing politics; rather, I wanted to emphasize the danger of his politics while also being able to empathize with his commitment.

I would have to be persuaded very strongly to work with Brian DePalma, because I think he's a sick misogynist. I wouldn't want to be part of something that perpetuates the violation of women with power tools. As long as movies promote thinking and not grazing, I think I would consider almost anything someone asked me to do. But there's a lot of garbage out there, and I won't be a part of that.

WHAT HAS BEEN YOUR BIGGEST SACRIFICE FOR SUCCESS?

I guess baseball, because I could be playing. That's not really a sacrifice, though. I feel it's a pretty good trade off. My time, effort and sweat are things one should aspire to; some people consider that a sacrifice—I don't.

HOW DOES YOUR IMAGE DIFFER FROM YOU AS A PERSON?

I was startled by a lot of interviews for *No Man's Land*. I felt I had a lot of responsibilities to promote the film, even though I didn't like the film. People had this perception of me that I was this "nice guy next door"; I guess my self-image is a little different from that. I think I have a more urban perspective, and I carry myself differently.

IS ACTING EVER A STRUGGLE FOR YOU?

When you're one of the aspiring actors in this world, you feel if you can just get that one job—just get discovered by somebody like Coppolla—everything will fall into place. When you discover that's not true, it's like discovering your parents are fallible. It's one of those important things that has to happen; it brings the hostilities of the universe into a brighter focus.

WHAT DO YOU LIKE BEST ABOUT SUCCESS?

I like not having to go in and humiliate myself in order to get a part. That whole process of auditioning is humiliating. Now people send me scripts, and if I'm interested, we take it from there. I don't have to go to cold readings. I'm a little concerned; I'm starting to get recognized now—it scares me a lot. I like to move

freely in public, and when people spot you, it can make you feel self-conscious. I remember when I first met Joe Namath—he was one of my heroes. He was so cool with me, and I remember that when I meet people. You try to be gracious.

IF YOU COULD STAR IN AN ONSCREEN BIOGRAPHY OF SOMEONE, WHO WOULD IT BE AND WHY?

I think I'd like to play Oliver North, because I'm afraid someone else will do it and make him into a hero.

WHO ARE SOME OF YOUR IDOLS OR HEROES?

Dwight Evans. Ralph Nader. A lot of my idols are in sports, like the guys who tough it out. Of my peers, I think Matthew Modine has done a lot of nice work. I really admire Christopher Walken, Robert De-Niro and Robert Duvall.

WHAT SPIRITUAL THINGS ARE IMPORTANT TO YOU?

The most spiritual thing that runs through my life is the work ethic. You work hard and you go home and try to be decent to the people around you. I don't have a specific spiritual orientation. I believe there's got to be some kind of prevailing force that calls the shots behind this madness.

WHAT SOCIAL CONCERNS DO YOU HAVE?

I'm really concerned with the systematic destruction of our planet, in terms of pollution. I think I'll try to have a positive influence by presenting ideas a certain way in my work—I can be more effective that way. I'd love to do a movie about the environmental movement of the seventies.

HOW DO YOU FEEL YOU FIT INTO THE CONTEXT OF THE NEW BREED?

I think that the unbridled optimism that's often been Hollywood's hallmark needs close examination. It's time for America to grow up and become an adult civilization. If there is a new breed and I am a part of that, the best thing that could happen would be to help people become more alert and realize what's going on in the world. To be a little bit more aware—turn off the TV and look out the window.

Donovan Leitch, Jr.

I led a pretty wild youth. I ran around with a bizarre group of kids, mostly black. I'd ditch school a lot, and I'd spend my lunch breaks, when I did go to school, walking down Hollywood Boulevard, so I guess I was exposed to a lot of weirdness at a very young age.

I was doing really poorly in school, and one day my guidance counselor suggested I put the same energy I'd been putting into ditching school and going to video arcades into attending drama class. I auditioned for a junior high school musical and really got into it—wild costumes, singing songs and everything.

One day PBS came to my school, scouting for a show called *K.I.D.S.*, about a bunch of kids who run a radio station. I got a bit part on the show—one line. I had a great time. When I got a check for $400 for one day's work, I knew I had found my career.

I then spent two years of auditioning for everything under the sun. From *ET* to *The Outsiders*, if a film had kids in it, I auditioned for it. I came really close on *Back to the Future* and on a lot of other things, but it took a really long time to get my name around. When you don't have any credits, it's hard for directors to want to hire you, because they think you're too inexperienced and that you won't deliver when you get in front of the camera.

Actors have to have a certain perspective about losing parts, though. You're rejected so many times a year, you have to come up with some set of excuses or else you become a completely insecure person. I say things like, "It wasn't meant to be," or, "Fate guided me to or from that role."

It's harder to accept the rejection, the closer you get to a part. You begin to get very excited, and sometimes the director, who doesn't always have the final say, will tell you that you're perfect and that you have the part. A week later, however, you find out that Rob Lowe got the part. Most of the time, they'll be behind you until you lose the role, and then they disappear.

I want to do roles that are both physically and emotionally challenging. I wouldn't want to play a part that's just like me, like Donovan; I think that's cheating myself. Plus, I don't think you want to let your audience know too much about you. That's the great thing about actors like Clark Gable and Humphrey Bogart—their private lives were a mystery. I want to get a few more films under my belt and have people say, "He was as great as Del Green," in *The In Crowd* or, "He was great as Peter Moran, in *And God Created Woman*, but I wonder what Donovan's like?"

Before I take a role, I consider what effect the film is going to have on the audience. A lot of kids watch films and take them very seriously. Some people say, "It's an acting part, it's a job, it's money," but I have to maintain a certain sense of morality and be smart. I'd love for all my roles to deal with modern-day problems that offer some sort of solution.

I'm unhappy with the world situation right now. I think it's ridiculous that we have enough bombs to blow up the world a hundred times over—that's a bit of an overkill. They can use the same money to improve education or feed the homeless or even find a cure for AIDS. I just think the money is being spent in the wrong places.

"Being an actor puts me in a position to make a difference. I'm involved with SANE and Young Artists United (a social action group comprised of young actors, writers, directors, etc., dedicated to helping kids deal with issues like suicide, child abuse and alcoholism). I'm also writing and co-producing *The Cousins Club* for Paramount.

If I can affect an audience by a film I've written or a part I've played in, that would make me really happy."

I had this girlfriend in high school named Ellen Boyle. We both went to the University of Michigan, but in college she was constantly putting me off. She was an actress, and I felt I had to do something to gain her respect, so the summer of my junior year, I enrolled at the American Conservatory Theater's summer workshop in San Francisco.

I figured if I went there, came back with a lot of really big stories and I was a cool actor, she would be more into me. It didn't work—she blew me off. It didn't matter though, because ACT changed my life—it was a real awakening for me. I was 21 years old, and for the first time I was really confronting myself on a lot of issues and letting myself experience a lot of emotions. That summer I discovered a positive vent for my feelings.

The following year, I applied to graduate schools, and I was accepted at the Yale School of Drama. I decided if I was going to go on and try to become an actor, I couldn't just go to New York or Los Angeles and try to learn by doing it. When you come from St. Clair Shores, Michigan, acting is the last profession you consider, and I didn't know where to begin. Besides it's not my style. I wanted to explore different possibilities and create a foundation.

In retrospect, the most important thing about Yale wasn't so much the training, the classroom efforts, as much as the efforts of just doing plays. I had the chance to do plays, start to finish, on every level—big theaters, small theaters, long rehearsal processes, short rehearsal processes. The whole thing added up to one large experience of what it was like to go through the production of a play from the first day of rehearsals to the strike [striking of the set].

I went through that process over 30 times in three years at Yale, which is a lot. I would never have been able to do that in New York City as a working actor. Even if I were, I would have been under a lot of pressure from producers, reviewers and fellow actors. Yale was like an incubator for my talent. It was completely free from outside forces, judgment or results; it allowed me to develop.

By the time I graduated, I had secured a role on *Ryan's Hope*. I started out as a day player—as "punk #1"—but instead of showing up in green sneakers and a red leather tie, daytime TV's version of what a punk should be, I showed up in a leather jacket, boots, black jeans, three earrings in each ear, studs on my fingers and around my wrists, and my hair was spray-painted black and spiked out.

At first they thought I had wandered in off the streets, but when they found out who I was, they were knocked out; they really liked me and they ended up writing in a part for me. I worked on the

Don Harvey

show for the entire summer. The only reason I got that job was because I did my preparation and I went in there with a fucking concept—something daytime TV is devoid of. That was my first gig.

Six months later, I replaced Aidan Quinn in Sam Shepard's "A Lie of The Mind" off Broadway. Since then, I've done five films including *Motherland* with Jason Patric and Steven Bauer and *Eight Men Out* with John Cusack and Charlie Sheen. At first film acting was a real struggle for me. I wasn't sure how much of my stage training was applicable. I've now learned to conserve my energy for the moments that count, to be selective and make choices rather than bang my head against the wall, digging through my entire range on every character.

Film and theater are very different. I think film is a medium that has more to do with personalities and really capturing a person in his natural element. It has to do with stripping yourself down and trying to be real. In theater, there is a lot of technique involved in getting across the edge of the stage and reaching into the audience. You have a gap there you have to get over. In film, the camera is reaching out to you.

If you are talking about acting as a tradition and a craft, film has only been around for 50 years. Before that, if you were an actor, you went out and worked onstage. In recording studios they can manipulate and alter a singer's voice to make him sound like someone else. The true test is when he walks out onstage and open his mouth and starts singing; then you know whether or not he can sing. It's the same thing with acting. A director can do so much with an actor's performance on film. You can do a scene a hundred times, and you can screw up every take but one. The director can then use a small part of that take and a small part of another take and put together a performance that is halfway decent. Your dignity and credibility as an artist are not truly on the line.

When you walk out onstage, however, *you* are the show; it doesn't matter what the director, the lighting designer or the set designer have done. They are all important, but once you're out onstage, it's just you and your audience. They can tell in a second if you're tense, if you feel like you're not comfortable there or if you're making a move that's inconsistent with the character you are playing. It's obvious: your whole body, every move you make, every time you breathe every time you go to pick something up.

I'm not saying that actors who only do film can't act—although most of them can't. It's just a different technique. I'm not saying one is more difficult than the other—if you are a good stage actor or a good film actor, you have different tasks ahead of you either way. The aspect of theatrical acting which you cannot get by doing film acting, however, is the start-to-finish performance of a piece. For two and a half hours, you go out

onstage and you are that character for the entire time. When you do a film there's no scene that lasts more than a minute or two, and that scene is usually split up into smaller segments. By the time you really start to relax, the scene is over.

Therefore, if you are an actor, the only way I feel you can seriously educate yourself is onstage. If you haven't done stage, you haven't entered the realm of the acting experience. More film actors should do theater. Many of them have the money, the name and the credibility, and, obviously they could create the opportunities if they wanted them; they just don't want to.

Theater is a humbling experience: there's not a lot of people around. You don't have craft service. There's no one to knock on your honey wagon door (trailer) to tell you you're up. It's just you. You go into a room with another actor, a stage manager and a director and rehearse a scene for five fucking hours. There's no real payoff except your own growth as an actor.

Most film actors are into immediate gratification. It's a long hard process to get to an opening night: a lot of criticism, a lot of self-study, a lot of input from the director. Most film actors just can't deal with it. Their thing is about getting that payment *now*. I love doing film; I'm beginning to work steadily in film and develop relationships. The difference is, I'm willing to wait for the big payoff. I'm willing to wait.

I've honed my craft to a point where I have the tools to draw from in creating and re-creating a moment. For me, there are no accidents.

David Lynch had been searching for the right actor to play the lead in his multi-million dollar science fiction epic *Dune* for months. After draining the overflowing acting pools of Los Angeles and New York City, he embarked on a nationwide casting search. It was during this talent hunt that David discovered Kyle MacLachlan, a neophyte actor from Seattle, Washington, whose previous experience had been limited to local theater.

David sensed and was able to draw on an intensity from the young actor that even Kyle was unaware he possessed. When *Dune* was not a box office success, however, Kyle returned to class and to the stage and worked on developing his newly discovered intensity into a craft. When David finally financed *Blue Velvet* (funding fell through after *Dune*'s poor performance), he once again cast Kyle as the film's lead, further developing a unique actor/director relationship.

Since *Blue Velvet*, Kyle says he has gotten in touch with his feelings and emotions. As an actor, he has grown as a result of working out inhibitions harbored since childhood, which he suppressed for so many years. Kyle looks forward to utilizing his newfound strength and awareness in his future roles.

Kyle MacLachlan

IF I WERE TO ASK ONE OF YOUR FRIENDS FROM HIGH SCHOOL WHAT YOU WERE LIKE, WHAT WOULD THEY SAY AND HOW WOULD THEY DESCRIBE YOU?

They would say I was unpredictable, spontaneous, talented and that I could laugh at myself. They would also say I was somebody who should have let his hair down a little bit more. I was under the gun of being well-behaved. My parents expected a certain kind of behavior of me. They insisted on their children being considerate and always aware of the *other* person. When you're growing up, you have to experience the extremes of adolescence. I don't think I was able to experience them the way I wanted to. From my point of view now, at 28, I realized I just wanted to tear the walls down, something I never felt I could do, and something which I'm discovering I can do now, at this late date. I think it's better to discover that at 28 than at 45 or 60.

SO WHAT ARE YOU DOING OR FEELING DIFFERENTLY?

I'm just trying to be aware when I hold feelings in and not feel guilt when I let them out. Or acknowledging a certain part of me—who I really am. A lot of my repression was sexual: I was being respectable; I was being very good. Now there is this need inside of myself to kind of explode sometimes. It's a good thing, and I don't mean by being sexually deviant or strange. I just want to acknowl-

edge part of me as a man, and it's going to make it interesting for Laura and I, because we've been together two years now and we're just beginning to explore new possibilities. Things have changed now that I don't feel I have to behave in a certain way because of what I learned as a child. It's time to find an acting role to reinforce that realization.

WHEN DID YOU START ACTING?

I did plays all through high school and at college. The first summer of college, I went away and did summer stock.

IS THEATER STILL IMPORTANT TO YOUR GROWTH AS AN ACTOR?

Yes, on so many different levels as a person and as an actor. I recently did "Romeo and Juliet" in North Carolina. Going back to the theater, I suddenly found myself in control of what I was doing, whereas I had never felt that with film. As Romeo, I was the one running the show—or at least that's how I felt.

HOW DO YOU FEEL ABOUT MOST OF THE SCRIPTS YOU ARE SUBMITTED?

I don't get a lot of scripts, because I'm picky and I'm on the fringe. My agency is huge, and the best scripts go to guys like Sean Penn—they command the most bucks and bring the most people into the movie theaters. If they don't like or are not interested in a script, *then* I might get to read it. Most of the scripts I get are borderline.

WHAT DO YOU LOOK FOR IN A SCRIPT?

I look for a story that's plausible and dialogue that's real. I look for scripts that have something to offer society. Sometimes you have to make compromises, though. I got to go off and do "Romeo," and I had a great fucking time, but I hardly made any money. I did *The Hidden* because I only had $3000 left in my bank account. I also did it because I saw good things in the movie, like the relationship between Michael Nouri and I, and how we grew to love each other. The movie turned out to be a lot of bullets, bodies, and death, and that pissed me off, so I refused to do any publicity for it. It was not the film the company told me they were going to make. That's why I have to do theater; otherwise I become a piece of meat, a piece of dust. This way I do something for myself and I don't have to be at the mercy of this machine.

WHAT WERE YOUR GOALS WHEN YOU FIRST STARTED OUT AND HOW HAVE THEY CHANGED?

At first I just wanted to be a solid regional-theater actor. Now I want to work with really good people, good directors. I want my audiences to feel like they're onscreen or onstage with me; I want people to be able to go through something in two hours and feel all the things I feel. I want to feel at one with my audience.

HOW DO YOU APPROACH A ROLE AND WHAT KIND OF PREPARATION DO YOU DO?

It's different every time. I try to understand my character—what he feels and why he does what he does. I try to truly get it on every level and have the whole thing make sense. A lot of stuff in *The Hidden, Dune,* and *Blue Velvet* didn't make sense to me, but I didn't have the strength, the power or the belief in myself to say, "No, we're going to make this work now and make my character into a real person."

DO YOU LOOK AT FILM AS A WAY TO SUPPORT YOURSELF AS A STAGE ACTOR?

No, they're both really important. Film demands are radically different from stage demands; I just haven't found film as fulfilling as being onstage. With theater, you've had a lot of time to flush your character out; you get to experience a whole row of things every night for two and a half hours. Usually the writing is somewhat superior, because it's stood the test of time, especially Shakespeare. You're dealing with stuff that moves the inner spirit so much more than film. With film, though, you've got these great little things to work on—it's all about detail. You can really construct an interesting character a little bit at a time. It's two different ways of putting together a person, and they're both very important.

DO YOU CONSIDER WHAT EFFECT A FILM WILL HAVE ON YOUR PEERS BEFORE ACCEPTING A ROLE?

Yeah. I thought a lot about *Blue Velvet* before I did it. That was a big decision; you've got to really think about what you're putting out there. I almost didn't do it, but I put my trust in David. I was offered a film about voodoo that is going to be filmed in Haiti, and I pulled out at the last minute after accepting it. There was something about it that didn't seem right, and I really do have a conscience.

AFTER YOU DID *DUNE*, DID IT GO TO YOUR HEAD AT ALL?

A little bit, yeah. When you hear, "You're going to be a major star and it's going to radically change your life," enough times, you start believing it's going to happen. After *Dune*, I was in Seattle doing theater, so I wasn't in L.A. the whole time the film was being hyped and set up. Because I wasn't part of the whole expectation, I didn't feel the crash as bad as I might have. I thought I was going to come into L.A. running at a high level, but I came back at the same level everyone else was at—the bottom. It was tough; I got down on myself for awhile, but then I just sort of shook it off. After *Dune*, we were supposed to go right into *Blue Velvet*, but it was cancelled because *Dune* was such a failure. I didn't work for a year, but I kept trying to walk the kind of path I wanted to walk, just being careful not to take any stuff that was easy.

WHAT HAS BEEN YOUR BIGGEST SACRIFICE FOR SUCCESS?

I don't think I've had to sacrifice anything. I look around and I see guys like Rob Lowe or Judd Nelson, and I see that they sacrifice a lot of privacy—but that's not something I've had to deal with. I can go anywhere and not be recognized unless someone is a *Dune* freak or a *Blue Velvet* freak. Success has just opened up things. I've met great people—I've met Laura.

WHAT IS THE DIFFERENCE BETWEEN YOU AS PERSON AND YOUR ONSCREEN IMAGE?

My image is a little cleaner than what I am inside. It's now up to me to let out that other part of myself, but it's hard.

IS BEING AN ACTOR EVER A STRUGGLE FOR YOU?

It's always a struggle—how can it *not* be? It's like holding a mirror to your face every day of your life, forcing self-examination. What else do you have besides yourself? Sure, you can blind yourself with shit and you can get yourself out of yourself, but in the end, who else do you turn around to face? To me, life is about self-discovery.

Acting is a great cause; it's the greatest profession because you're dealing with yourself all the time, and it kind of supports that self-discovery process.

IF YOU COULD STAR IN AN ONSCREEN BIOGRAPHY OF SOMEONE, WHO WOULD IT BE AND WHY?

There are a lot of people who have qualities I dream of or aspire to that I would like to experience. I'd like to play Rasputin; he was a pretty amazing fellow. There must have been a lot going on in this guy's mind to make him so powerful, and that's the side of him I'd like to explore.

WHAT SPIRITUAL THINGS ARE IMPORTANT TO YOU?

I think the source of creativity is a divine thing inside of ourselves. Acting from that source of creativity is a spiritual thing. I think having a great respect for that source in every person, including myself, acknowledging that divine quality and being honest and truthful to it is important.

WHAT IS YOUR BIGGEST FEAR?

My biggest fear has something to do with failure. Failure or the fear of not being worthy or being humiliated.

WHAT SOCIAL ISSUES ARE IMPORTANT TO YOU?

The whole nuclear thing is so fucking insane. Why create something that, if it gets into the wrong hands, could mean the end of everything for all of us? That's bullshit. Last May I went to Mercury, Nevada, with some protestors. We hung out and filmed the Mother's Day protest, and people crossing the lines of the base. I was glad I took part in that.

HOW DO YOU FEEL YOU FIT INTO THE CONTEXT OF THE NEW BREED?

There's sort of a sense of responsibility among a lot of young actors today. You do something like a sexploitation film and there's a whole karma thing attached to it—you're setting yourself up. I'm not into that. I give too much blood when I do a film—three months of my life. I might as well do things I can get behind. After all, isn't that the goal, ultimately?

Laura Dern

Laura Dern plays a lot of different roles in life. To those who have seen her critically acclaimed portrayal of the blind girl in *Mask*, she is a "white dove"—sensitive, spiritual, searching and, in a lot of ways, naive. To others, she is the daughter of Bruce Dern and Diane Ladd, coming of age onscreen in the film version of Joyce Carol Oates' *Smooth Talk*. To still others, she is the real-life and sometimes celluloid lover of actor Kyle MacLachan.

Through the roles she plays and the life she leads, Laura feels she is all of these things and more. She feels that the best thing about being an actress is getting to be different people and, while discovering things about them, also having the opportunity to explore and discover who *she* is.

TELL US ABOUT WHERE YOU GREW UP.

I grew up in Los Angeles, in a suburb near Coldwater Canyon that had a middle-class feel to it. The houses surrounding mine were one- and two-story colonials. I remember that wonderful brisk feeling after it would rain—otherwise there was smog. My room was my place, my solace. Ours was an all-female house—my mother, my grandmother and me. I was a creative child—a little confused but always searching.

WHAT WERE YOU LIKE IN HIGH SCHOOL?

I was very busy with acting, school and participating in student government. I was very political and very liberal—one could have a great argument with me. I was sort of on my own, kind of independent. I was an actress.

WHEN DID YOU DECIDE YOU WANTED TO BECOME AN ACTRESS?

When I was nine. I had done a little extra work, and after Marty Scorsese complimented me on being able to sustain 20 takes of licking an ice cream cone, I was hooked. My parents tried to show me the hardships of acting, but their understanding of their craft, combined with their passion for it, was such a beautiful thing that it overshadowed the struggle. When I told my mom I wanted to become an actress, she said: "If you want to do it, you're going to have to do it on your own. And you've got to study for at least two years before you start auditioning."

I went to the Lee Strasberg Institute in Los Angeles. When I was 11, I met an agent at the house of a family friend. I told this woman my parents wouldn't help me but that I really wanted to be an actress. She told me to come to her office to do a monologue for her. After I did, she sent me up for this movie called *Foxes*. I lied and told the casting director I was 14, but felt I could play 17. I screentested for the director, who thought I looked too young, but he liked me and wanted me to be in the movie. I had two scenes and worked a week and a half. That was my first job, and from then on, I dedicated myself to my career.

WHAT WERE YOUR GOALS WHEN YOU FIRST STARTED OUT AND HOW HAVE THEY CHANGED?

When I first got the idea in my head that I wanted to act, my goals were pure. I think children have that purity, that desire to discover. So much comes into play with the games we learn to play and the egos we develop as we get older. I try to maintain that desire—to want to make people laugh, to make people cry. I want to explore those sides of myself, those different people inside of me.

WHY DO YOU THINK PEOPLE DEVELOP EGOS AS THEY GET OLDER?

As a teenager, producers, directors and casting agents would tell me, "We don't want you—we want her because she's prettier," or "she looks more right for the part," or "she's a better actress"—whatever their thing was that day. Insecurities creep in; egos creep in. You can really get trapped into that. Suddenly you find yourself acting because you want attention—to be in the limelight and to be worthy. You want to be accepted. It's easy to get trapped. I had to fight that.

DOES IT PUT ANY PRESSURE ON YOU THAT BOTH OF YOUR PARENTS ARE SUCCESSFUL ACTORS?

It does, but it also works to my benefit a

lot. There have been lots of times where I've walked into an office, and somebody has said, "Sure, I'd love to meet Bruce Dern's daughter." That may get me in the door, but it never gets me the part—ever. I've also walked into auditions and the director has said, "Sure, I've worked with your father," with such hatred. It works both ways.

HOW DO YOU FEEL ABOUT MOST OF THE SCRIPTS YOU ARE SUBMITTED?

The worst! So many people get caught up in what's salable and marketable. How are you going to know what's salable unless you try it. If it's different, how are you going to know if it's going to work or not unless people see it? The studios buy what's been proven, whether it's Sly Stallone or whatever the fad is at the moment. I get sick of seeing trends in scripts. I love seeing people doing things that are different—just simple stories, just truth.

WHAT DO YOU LOOK FOR IN A SCRIPT?

I look for truth. When I start hearing words out of characters that are not believable, then how could I say them? I really care about the state of the world right now, and I look for scripts that will make a difference, even if it's a small one.

DO YOU CONSIDER WHAT EFFECT A FILM WILL HAVE ON YOUR PEERS WHEN TAKING A ROLE?

Yes. So many times I think about the masses, not just my peers. The film Smooth Talk I felt was a really important movie for people my age. No one had ever looked at a young girl's sexuality on film like that before. I had to think for a long time whether to do Blue Velvet or not; my morals really came into it. Ultimately, my trust in David Lynch won out—I just think his vision is fantastic. When I read the script of Blue Velvet, I really wanted Sandy to have some strength so that the audience could see the light in the darkness.

IS STUDYING IMPORTANT TO YOUR GROWTH AS AN ACTRESS?

Studying is really important to me. I've been studying since before I started working. The more I work, though, the more excited I get about all the things I can learn. The more you learn about yourself through studying, the more pure you become. The more pure you become, the more pure you can be onscreen, the more honest you can be. To me, learning about yourself and learning about acting is the same thing, it's working on sensory things; it's knowing how to recall textures—to be able to go back to how you felt, so that when you're on a set, you can be honest in your performance. When making a film, there's so much make-believe around you, it's hard to be honest a lot of the time.

WHAT HAS BEEN YOUR BIGGEST SACRIFICE FOR SUCCESS?

College. Sometimes I just want to be a person having fun and going to school, going crazy over midterms and leading that kind of life. I feel guilty about not going to college. I went to UCLA for two days before I got Smooth Talk and to USC for two months before I got Blue Velvet.

IS BEING AN ACTRESS EVER A STRUGGLE FOR YOU?

Yes. I love to read, paint and go horseback riding, and there's no time to do those things right now. Eventually I'll want a family and children, and coordinating that with my career will be a struggle. I also want to be involved with the future of the world—I'm real scared about our future. I'm afraid about what could happen on a nuclear level—it's becoming such a reality.

WHAT SPIRITUAL THINGS ARE IMPORTANT TO YOU?

Learning to come from a place of love, learning to be satisfied with myself, feeling worthy and, in my acceptance, being able to share that with other people. That's a major battle, but that's my goal—I want to get in touch with that side of myself. I need to become grounded in a sense of myself where it's quiet and at peace.

IF YOU COULD STAR IN AN ONSCREEN BIOGRAPHY OF SOMEONE, WHO WOULD IT BE AND WHY?

Monet, but I'm not an old man. He just enjoyed the simplicity of life so much. I'd really like to play someone who's constantly discovering life through simplicity.

IF YOU COULD REMAKE ANY MOVIE, WHAT WOULD IT BE AND WHY?

Stage Door is pretty incredible. I'd love to do any of the parts in that film. The beauty of that movie was that actresses like Katharine Hepburn, Ann Miller and Lucille Ball were all in it before they were famous. I love Katharine Hepburn—she's perfect.

WHAT ARE YOU DOING TO MAKE A DIFFERENCE?

I'm involved in groups like SANE, and I try to state my case in interviews and hope people will listen.

WHY DO YOU THINK THERE ARE NO LONGER ANY LEADING LADIES IN HOLLYWOOD, THE WAY THERE WERE IN THE DAYS OF THE STUDIO SYSTEM?

During that period, actresses made many movies—they had the opportunity to show a lot of different sides of themselves. Today, leading ladies have to do more with fewer films. Actresses like Jessica Lange, Meryl Streep and Sissy Spacek are under unbelievable pressure to produce.

WHO IS THE IDEAL LEADING MAN YOU COULD BE CAST OPPOSITE?

I got my wish once—Kyle MacLachlan. Kyle reminds me of Cary Grant. I'd like to be able to play opposite him again in a Hepburn-Tracy kind of movie. We are really funny together. I love great acting; I love to go to the movies and say that a certain actor was brilliant. I want to work with everybody who's great. I'd also like to work with my parents.

IF THERE ARE TWO OTHER ACTRESSES UP FOR A ROLE, AND ALL OF YOU ARE EQUAL IN TERMS OF LOOKS, TALENT, ETC., WHY SHOULD A DIRECTOR CHOOSE YOU OVER THE OTHER TWO ACTRESSES?

Because I'm different. I would commit. I could guarantee a hundred-percent commitment, whereas some actresses are not ready to do that.

HOW DO YOU FEEL YOU FIT INTO THE CONTEXT OF THE NEW BREED?

I feel I am the kind of actress who can enjoy acting without falling victim to the business. Politically and socially, the world is now a new place because of everything from AIDS to nuclear arms to teenagers being stars of movies. Maybe the new breed can be a conscious one, a caring one. That would be really nice and an honor to be part of.

As usual, the front door to Ione Skye's house is wide-open, the screen door slightly ajar, so the calico cats, lounging lazily on the front porch, can enter and exit without a problem. There is always an open-door policy at the Hollywood Hills home Ione shares with her brother, actor Donovan Leitch, Jr., and her mother and stepfather, Enid and Billy Karl. A self-proclaimed ex-flower child, Enid has carried over the values of harmony and unconditional love into her family's everyday living environment.

As a result, stepping into Ione's house is almost like falling into a time warp. A feeling of trust and tranquility is immediately apparent, as is an overwhelming sense of the love of life and living in the here and now. Photos of Ione and Donovan at various ages and stages hang everywhere, and sixties relics like old concert posters and albums clutter the living room.

One musician's albums you're not likely to find in this house are those of Ione's father, folk-rock troubadour Donovan. Enid and Donovan, Sr., split up (they lived together but were never married) before Ione was born, and the actress has never met her father.

As a child, Ione describes herself as being painfully shy and quiet, her hair constantly hanging in front of her face so she wouldn't have to look at or talk to anyone. Since her onscreen debut in *River's Edge*, however, Ione says she feels more comfortable with herself and, as a result, more comfortable around other people. Like a flower, Ione is opening up, becoming increasingly more beautiful and blossoming into a talented actress.

Ione Skye

HOW WERE YOU DISCOVERED FOR *RIVER'S EDGE*?

Amy Etra, a photographer friend of my mom's, was doing a fashion layout for *L.A. Weekly*, and she needed a female model. She asked me to come over to her house and try on a dress. The dress fit, so I wore it, but because I was so made up, people didn't even recognize me; I didn't recognize myself. A few weeks later, my mother told me a director had seen my picture in the paper and wanted me to read for this film. I was so nervous, I didn't want to do it, but I ended up going to the audition thinking nothing would happen.

WHY DID YOU CHANGE YOUR MIND AND GO TO THE AUDITION?

Because mother, who is as shy as I am said, 'Listen, the worst thing that could happen is that you'll end up in the same place you're in right now.' I thought about it and decided to give it a shot. I auditioned, got called back five times—including a screen test with Crispin [Glover] and Keanu [Reeves]—and I finally got the part.

HOW DID YOU FEEL AFTER GETTING CAST IN THE FIRST FEATURE FILM FOR WHICH YOU AUDITIONED?

I was really nervous. The first day on the set, I thought I was going to faint or just turn around and run away. I felt physically ill. All of the other actors had already done movies, and I thought they were going to think less of me because I was just starting out. I also had mixed feelings because I didn't know if I really liked acting or not. Now, when I act, I love it—it's just something that's a lot of fun. Then, it made me so nervous, I couldn't have any fun.

WHEN DID THE NERVOUSNESS GO AWAY?

It hasn't gone away yet—it's still there. I use it differently now, though, and it doesn't make me feel sick when I'm acting.

IS YOUR CHARACTER IN RIVER'S EDGE DIFFERENT FROM YOU?

For a long time, I thought I was playing her just like myself, but when I saw the film for the first time, I thought, 'No, that's not me, and that's not what I'll ever be like.' My character didn't have the family support I have. She didn't know that if she didn't like high school, she could do other things. I always knew that. I know that if I choose to write or draw or act instead of going to high school, my parents will still support and love me. She didn't do the high school thing, and she had nothing to fall back on. She had no future.

SO YOUR MOTHER AND BILLY ENCOURAGE YOUR CREATIVITY?

Definitely. I've been really lucky. My mother has always been wonderful and has made me feel nothing I did was weird. I never thought I was normal, and she made that seem OK. We can talk about anything. Her attitude is, accept it and laugh about it. She buys me paint sets and things. She encouraged me with my schoolwork, like everyone else's parents, but she was never flipped out about school. She wanted me to do well for myself and get as much as possible out of it, but she made me realize it wasn't the most important thing in the world. I've always read a lot, written stories and drawn, and she encouraged me with those things. My mom is really special.

YOU'VE NEVER MET YOUR FATHER?

No. I had a dream that I saw him and I walked right past him. I was kind of hiding because I didn't want to meet him. When I was little, I had a chance to meet him, but I was too shy. I didn't know what to say to him. I don't think I want to ever meet him; I'd like to think I don't *have* a father. For some reason, it just makes me feel better.

DO YOU HAVE A HARD TIME DEALING WITH PEOPLE WHO IDENTIFY YOU AS DONOVAN'S DAUGHTER WHEN YOU'VE NEVER EVEN MET YOUR FATHER AND WHEN THE REAL SUPPORT IN YOUR LIFE COMES FROM YOUR MOTHER?

Yes. I don't know why people do that, but I do believe that part of each of your parents is really in you, not only physically but in every other way. I think people are interested in your experiences when you're born in the public eye. People want to know how your parents brought you up, what they exposed you to, who their friends and lovers were and things like that.

HAS BEING AN ACTRESS EVER BEEN A STRUGGLE FOR YOU?

It's only been hard because I get so critical of myself. I know a lot of actresses who find their entire career to be a struggle, but if it became too hard, I just wouldn't do it. I get frustrated about my work. I just want it to be good. I'm also concerned about what other young actors and actresses will think about me. When older people say, 'Oh, she's really good,' it's different than getting praise from my peers. They're more qualified to judge, because they're at the same point I am. I've been lucky: I've worked almost non-stop since I started, so that part of my career has not been a struggle at all.

HOW DO YOU PREPARE FOR A PART?

I still don't know much about that sort of thing. I don't have any methods or anything like that. I've tried a lot of different things on my own, though. For *River's Edge* I tried thinking of friends I knew, but for *Jimmy Reardon* and *Napoleon and Josephine*, I didn't do any heavy-duty preparation.

SO YOU JUST STUDIED YOUR SCRIPT?

Yes. I think talking with other actors is the best way to prepare. In *Napoleon and Josephine*, Armand Assante, who played Napoleon, really helped me. With *Jimmy Reardon*, we were all so close offscreen, we would go over the scenes beforehand, and that helped a lot.

WHAT KIND OF ROLES ARE YOU LOOKING FOR NOW?

I don't want to play another bitch. In *Jimmy Reardon* and *Napoleon and Josephine* I play exaggerated roles; now I want to play something more real. I still feel I'm not ready to tackle a lot of roles. I'm kind of a wimp in that way. I love fairytales like Cocteau's *Beauty and the Beast*. In the future I would love to do one if it were properly done. I don't care if the movies I do are huge at the box offices. I want to be respected. I don't care if people say 'who?' when they hear my name, as long as some day I gain their respect as a serious actress.

WHEN YOU TAKE A PART, DO YOU CONSIDER WHAT EFFECT IT WILL HAVE ON YOUR PEERS?

Yes. I would never do a film that had a lot of violence. I don't like violence. I wouldn't do a film like *Top Gun*, where they could stand outside movie theaters and sign people up for the army. I would do nothing to support that. I also wouldn't do a movie where kids were doing drugs and it was glamourized.

ARE YOU ANTI-DRUG?

Well, they're not something I need. They're actually something no one needs. In the seventies, kids got together and did drugs, and then ended up crying and releasing everything together. I hope kids today know they don't need drugs to do that.

WHAT DO KIDS TODAY NEED TO RELEASE?

It could be anything—boredom, fear, anger. A lot of things are really scary in life, but you don't need drugs to get through it. You just need to know you're good at something, and not be afraid to succeed at it. Kids today are really angry, and it's really hard to help someone who is angry and doesn't love himself. Even little kids I meet are really angry. They play with toy guns, and they want you to pretend like you're dead. I want to hug them and say, 'Listen, I love you,' but they don't want to hear that. It's hard because they are the ones who really need it.

WHAT'S YOUR BIGGEST FEAR?

There are so many things right now that I find really scary. The world is so violent—that's scary. I hope AIDS goes away—that's a fear for everyone. It's not fair that it has to be something sexual. People should be able to make love without worrying about it. I think people need to concentrate more on dealing with people. The world is too technical now. People seem to be more concerned with building new things than building families.

WHAT ARE YOU DOING TO MAKE A DIFFERENCE?

I'm involved with a group called Young Artists United. It's wonderful because they take issues like bulimia, drugs, suicide, AIDS, anything, and then go to schools around the country to talk to kids about them. The best thing about it is that it's young people communicating with other young people. Kids look up to their idols, and we make a difference.

DO YOU BELIEVE THAT SOMETHING MORE POWERFUL THAN YOURSELF IS GETTING YOU TO WHERE YOU'RE GOING?

I don't think so. I think you make your own rules in life. There's a reason for everything that happens to you, but the most important thing in life is for you to like yourself. It sounds weird, but it's very important. I think if there were reincarnation, the lesson you'd keep coming back to learn is to love yourself, 'cause then, and only then, can you love everyone else.

HOW DO YOU FEEL YOU FIT INTO THE CONTEXT OF *THE NEW BREED?*

I'm part of a whole new generation of actors. We think of acting as an art form; at least the people I know who are actors are very concerned with their craft.

LIKE WHO?

Well, like River Phoenix and Martha Plimpton, and all the people I've worked with that are up-and-coming people. We're approaching acting and making movies like Luis Bunnel did in the seventies, or how Salvador Dali approached painting—we're into it for the sake of making art. Nothing else matters; our whole thing is creating.

Courteney Cox

My parents got divorced when I was ten; I was in camp. Even though I knew they were separated, the divorce really upset me. When I got home from camp, my brother and I tried to set my parents up on dinner dates. He'd take my father out and I'd take my mother out, and we'd meet at Wendy's. We tried everything, but nothing worked.

My dad moved from where we lived in Birmingham, Alabama, to Florida, and my mom got only $400 a month from him for alimony and child support. We didn't have a lot of money to buy clothes or to do what we wanted to do. I got very resentful towards my mother, and, as a result, very independent.

I got my first job after school when I was 13, because I wanted to buy clothes and save money for a car. I called names out of the phone book to raise money for the retardation foundation. I was very ambitious. All through high school, I took a full load of classes and worked 40 hours a week.

My mother remarried, and my stepfather's nephew is Miles Copeland, who owns I.R.S. Records and managed the Police. Whenever the band would come to Birmingham, Miles would fly down for the show and stay at our house. He'd always say, "Courteney, you've got to get out of here—you're too ambitious to stay in Birmingham. You're going to have to leave at some point, so why don't you come to New York." I'd laugh at him and say that that was a nice dream, but to get real.

My senior year in high school, the Police played a big show in an arena in Birmingham. When Miles came down, he invited me to come to a Police concert in New York two weeks later and said he would take me for an interview at the Ford modeling agency. I was very excited, but I wondered how he was going to get me in. I'm only 5'5", and it wasn't like they were excited to meet girls from Alabama who had never done anything aside from ads for a local department store.

He got me the interview by bribing an agent with two free Police tickets for that night's sold-out show in New York. When they met me, they thought I was too short, but decided to send me out on two interviews anyway. I lucked out—one of my interviews was at *Young Miss* magazine, and I booked the job that day. When I graduated from high school a few weeks later, I moved to New York.

I didn't have a dime, and at first I slept on different people's floors. When I had finally saved enough money to be able to afford an apartment, I moved to the Upper West Side, where I shared a one-bedroom apartment. The rent's so expensive in New York, all the money I made went to pay for my apartment. My best friend lived downstairs; I used to call her up and say, "I don't have any money, but do you want to have dinner?" Then I'd bring down a can of tomato soup, a loaf of bread and a tub of Knudson's whipped butter. I'd have six slices of bread and butter and a bowl of tomato soup. Besides a can of tuna once in a while, that's all I ate for nine months. But I was ambitious and I wanted to succeed.

I hated modeling—I wasn't tall enough or beautiful enough to become a real model—and once I got my first commercial, I quit. I started taking acting classes and speech lessons to lose my southern accent. My real break came when I got the Bruce Springsteen "Dancing in the Dark" video. Brian DePalma cast me over a couple of hundred other girls. He wanted someone who could look surprised when Bruce pulled them out of the audience take after take, but he wasn't looking for Meryl Streep.

After that I was flown out to L.A. to screen test for *Code Name Foxfire*, which I didn't get, but I did end up getting "*Misfits of Science*," which I auditioned for because by chance someone had walked me over to that set after my screen test. After doing *Masters of the Universe*, some TV guest roles and a TV movie for NBC, I got *Family Ties*.

Laura, my character on "*Family Ties*," seems like an easy role to play, but she and I are so completely opposite. I'm amazed at the words that come out of her mouth sometimes. It's strange my friends see me on the show and say, "You would never have done that at all," and I explain it's a role—I'm not playing Courteney Cox.

Family Ties is going to last one more season, and I'm now looking for dramatic roles. A lot of people put down television, but working in front of an audience of 300 people every week has been an incredible learning experience for me. There are so many levels of success, and right now I'm at the bottom, if you're talking about *success* success. My goal right now is to just get through each day, try to keep my eyes open and learn as much as I can. I still have a lot I want to accomplish, because I'm by no means where I want to be yet as an actress.

Larry Fishburne

I grew up at 19 Fiske Place in Brooklyn, New York. To get to my apartment, you had to climb up three flights of cold, dark, gray marble steps. I remember having to walk up those steps in front of my mother sometimes when I was bad at school; it would be like the longest walk in the world.

We lived in Apartment 3C. Our bedrooms faced the street, and at three in the afternoon, you could always hear the kids out playing stickball, roller hockey, tag or whatever. My house was always filled with the incredible aromas of African-American cuisine—fried chicken, chitlins, greens, grits, biscuits, bacon and, occasionally, lasagna. I had an Italian friend whose house I would go to for dinner a lot, and I grew very fond of lasagna, so my mother would make it once in a while.

My parents had separated when I was three and had gotten divorced when I was ten. I was an only child. I saw my dad at least once a month on a Sunday, and we would go to the movies. When I came back to the neighborhood at 6 p.m., I'd act out the movie I'd seen that afternoon for all the kids on the block. Most of them came from large families, so they couldn't afford to go to the movies. That was my first experience with acting.

I've been acting professionally since I was 10, but I didn't start to take it seriously until I was 16 or 17. Up until the point, acting was something I enjoyed and was good at, and it was also a way for me to survive. I'm not a very physical person, and growing up where I grew up, there was ample opportunity to get into physical confrontations with people. Instead of saying, "Well, I'm just gonna kick your ass," I'd use my acting prowess and fuck them up *mentally*.

The experience that changed the way I looked at acting was working on *Apocalypse Now* with Francis Ford Coppolla. I began to look at acting as an art form. Francis looks at film as something that hasn't even begun to have been tapped the way it ought to be. The film business—i.e., Hollywood—hasn't utilized the medium to its fullest potential, and that subsequently has robbed cats like me and other young actors of the possibility of doing wonderful things with a new art form.

There is also a peculiar problem I have to deal with every day of my life. The problem is called racism, and regardless of all the wonderful work I have done and will do, the fact remains I am an African-American—I'm a black person. There are hundreds of scripts that go to white actors that I will never see. The majority of stuff I get sent on says "BLACK," which is why I don't get submitted piles of scripts—there are just not that many of them.

I don't have the flexibility to look for certain kinds of roles. If I'm available to go out and do a role, what I try to do is make sure my vibe is a vibe that any young black American or black man on the planet can relate to in a certain way. That I do because, after all, that's what I represent on the screen. Racism is a bitch. It exists and I just have to do the best I can.

When I got back from *Apocalypse Now*, I was 17, and everyone said, "Larry, you'll work all the time." If I had been a white boy, I'd be making more than Charlie Sheen, based on talent alone. That really fucked me up for a while, but I go with it. At least I'm working.

When a cat sits down to write a screenplay, he's concerned with his story and his primary characters. The rest of it is not as well thought out. For a white cat to write a story that has black characters in it, there's no telling how much he knows about black people. Once upon a time I used to shake my head, and go, this is bullshit. I don't expect him to have a clue anymore. How could he have a clue? Since I have all of the baggage with that, I just bring my bags.

To make it as a black actor, you have to work hard, stick around and deal with people as people. It can be really frustrating sometimes. I used to deal with my frustrations by getting fucked up a lot, but now, I just work through things and try not to let it interfere with my work. It's like that line in *Harvey*, when Jimmy Stewart says, "You can be oh so smart, or oh so pleasant." At work I try to be oh so pleasant; in life I try to be oh so smart.

Working with Spike Lee on *School Daze*, I got the chance to be pleasant and smart. Spike passed me the ball and said, "Run with it, homeboy." The film is about black people, and there *is* a difference. Aside from pigmentation, there are cultural differences—language, speech patterns, body language. All black people don't talk the same; there are cultural differences among all of us. It was my first opportunity as an actor to really let loose.

There's a possibility that *School Daze* will open up a lot of doors for me, but there's also the possibility people will say, "That was nice—next." I'm prepared for that. I'm still prepared to play the third character in someone else's movie. It really doesn't matter because I'm about my craft. That's what I take seriously.

Actors I know and I sit around all the time and have discussions about acting and about this one and that one. "That cat," we say, "is weak." Why? "Because he's not about the craft. He's about that other starry-eyed shit." That's not to say I don't like it when people get what I'm trying to do. I like it when I meet my brother in the street, and that cat says, "My brother—I like what you're doing in the movies."

My biggest fear is becoming very successful and recognizable and not knowing how to handle it. That's another reason I've always been into being an actor as opposed to wanting to become a star. The reason it's important to me that my people recognize me is that people of African descent in this country, and in a lot of countries around the world, get bombarded with negative images of themselves. That goes back to, "Why does the black man always have to play the pusher, the pimp and the so and so?" The reality is a lot of us still do that. I fight racism by trying to be right as rain and by promoting a positive self-image. That's what I'm doing to make a difference in the movies; that's what I'm doing to make a difference in the world.

Rodney Harvey

I grew up in a very street-oriented neighborhood in South Philadelphia. I was an angry kid, negative about everything. I hadn't seen my father in years; he abandoned my mother, my brothers and I when I was ten, and I was experiencing a lot of pain. I dealt with my problems by hanging out with my friends in an abandoned parking lot—drinking beers, smoking pot, snorting cocaine and taking valiums and tuinals.

I used to get into trouble with the cops for fighting and cutting class. Finally, I got busted for skipping school for six months—I just didn't want to go. My mother was married to a doctor at the time, so she sent me to a rich kids' reform school called St. Michaels. I lived there for a year, went to school and did all the things young teenage boys are supposed to do.

When the year was up, I went back to Philadelphia. Everything was fine until my grandfather died. Of 15 grandchildren, I was his favorite; he and I were very close. I loved him more than my mom. Once again, I dealt with my pain by doing drugs. This time, though, my mom flipped out and wanted to send me to a *real* reform school, so I ran away to New York City.

I had been in New York for six days and I was shopping in the Village when some guy walked up to me and asked me if I wanted to buy a switchblade. I said sure, handed him 20 bucks and he took off with my money. I chased after him, caught him, threw him on the ground and got my money back. That's when Paul Morrissey walked up to me and asked me if I wanted to audition for *Mixed Blood*, a film he was directing. I did, and he gave me the part of a street kid who helps run a kids' drug ring in the East Village.

Since then I've done six movies in three years. It's been hard for me, though, because only two of these films have been released. One was never finished, two couldn't find distribution and one has been in post-production forever. It's frustrating. I feel fortunate to have worked so much, but the films I've done are not the kind of films I want to be doing. It's work and it's experience, but I want to stop doing films where I only play the tough little street kid.

I've been on my own since I was 16, and at first I was impressed with going out to clubs and eating dinner in fancy restaurants; I got caught up in all the bullshit. I used to go to Helena's [a private club in Los Angeles] a lot, and it was like being in a movie. Everyone you would see up on screen was there getting drunk. I don't care about being glamorous, showing off what I'm wearing, who I'm with or the car I'm driving. After a while, I realized Helena's wasn't going to benefit me or help me to get a movie. My self-destructive days are over.

At first, I thought my career was a big joke, but recently I've gotten really serious about it. Getting roles has never been a problem for me, but now I'm going to be much more selective about what parts I take. I am going to start playing characters where I can show off my acting abilities. I may not be good at math or science, but I do know about life and what *I* want to do in life, and I think I have a lot to offer.

I wish I'd gone to school and gotten a great education. I wish I hadn't gotten into so many fights and been arrested. I wish everything was alright with my family and my father was living at home with my mother. Everything about Philadelphia disappoints me, but I'm not going to let it affect the rest of my life. I'm just now learning to trust people and to receive their trust, friendship and love. This is a big step for me. I can now tell who's good and who's bad. I have great instincts.

I've also used my instincts to guide my career so far. I never decided to become an actor—it was a gift given to me. I love acting; I want to be a great actor. I don't care about being rich and famous. I like to be good at whatever I do, and if I'm going to be an actor, I just want to be great at it. I wouldn't want to be a part of something like the "brat pack." Their movies don't really mean anything. They seem to be in it for the money and to be popular.

Johnny Depp

I went to Mirimar High School in Mirimar, Florida. People would remember me as the kid with the long hair who was always playing guitar. I used to bring my guitar to school, skip certain classes and sneak into the guitar class. The teacher would put me into a practice room and I'd play for hours. That's pretty much how I spent my high school years.

When I graduated, I moved to Los Angeles with a band I was playing with called the kids. We played around at the clubs on Sunset Strip a lot. One night, a friend of mine introduced me to Nicholas Cage. We started hanging out, and Nick suggested I try acting. At the time, I wasn't making much money with the band, so I decided to give it a shot.

He introduced me to his agent; she sent me out on an audition. The director gave me a script and told me to study it; I did, came back two days later, read for the part and they gave it to me. That was my first film—*Nightmare on Elm Street*.

At first it was all just trial by fire. I had never acted before, not even in school plays, and it was a tremendous challenge. I had to learn to hit marks, say lines and interact with other people, all at the same time. I also had to lose my inhibitions—I was terrified of making myself vulnerable; I knew nothing of it. It was the total opposite of being in a rock & roll band. In a band you have four people and you're all working to achieve whatever—a record deal, great songs, great gigs. With acting, I found it was just me, and it all depended on me. I had to make my own choices.

After *Elm Street*, I did a terrible sexploitation film called *Private Resort*. I did it because I needed the money badly and, at that point, I couldn't afford to be choosey; I figured at least I was earning my living by acting, and that beat working at Burger King or McDonalds. The film was a piece of shit, but I knew it would give me the opportunity to experiment and see how far I could go before pissing off the director and producer. For them it was a teenage exploitation film; for me it was an opportunity to learn—and to get *paid* for learning.

The major turning point of my career came when I did *Platoon*. Even though a lot of what I did was cut out, it was still one of the best experiences of my life. When you're taken out of your everyday life of trying to get a job and this and that, and you're put into a situation where you're living with 30 other guys in the jungle of a country you know nothing about, and you're living on rations, you become incredibly tight—like brothers. We watched each other's backs, and overall it was a very strange experience.

When I got back, I was very depressed. After being in the jungle for two and a half months with those guys and working on a project like that, coming back to life in L.A. was very difficult. On a smaller scale, I think it was a lot like what the soldiers felt coming back from Vietnam: One day they were in the jungle fighting with their buddies, trying to save their ass, and two days later they're walking down La Cienaga Boulevard looking for a hot dog.

I drank a lot. I played with a rock & roll band again for a while. I drank more and I got more depressed. I missed my buddies, and everyone had gone their own way. Finally I started to audition again, and it was about six months later that I got 21 *Jump Street*.

Television is a grind. It does not allow for experimentation—you don't have enough time to do much more than learn your lines and get to the set. Comparing the experience of doing film to television is like comparing Le Dome to McDonalds. If you go into Le Dome, you're going to get a great steak, fresh vegetables, a nice bottle of wine and you're going to sit and enjoy your meal for a few hours. You go to McDonalds and you're getting what you're asking for—a cheeseburger, fries and coke. Middle America wants McDonalds every night, so that's what they get. It's terrible.

If I have to do television, I'm glad it's on 21 *Jump Street*, because at least the show possesses a sense of honesty and confronts serious social issues like suicide, drugs and child abuse. At least there's potential there to help somebody. Whatever I'm doing must, in one way or another, possess a sense of truth. I can't force something out that's not honest to me. In any character I play, be it a rapist or a priest, there must be some element about that person inside of me that can come out. Otherwise it won't work—it's just a lie.

The best part of doing television is that it has increased my visibility in the business. The worst part is that I have to spend nine months out of the year in a hotel room in Vancouver, British Columbia, and that I have to sacrifice a lot of my free time and privacy. It's weird when people get your number and start calling you up to say you were rude to them because you didn't write to them or send them a picture, or that they are going to throw themselves off of the top of city hall because you haven't called them.

I got this letter from this girl who told me she was going to commit suicide if I didn't write her to help her with her problems. A lot of people told me to let it go because it probably was just bullshit—but who can take that chance? You never know.

I wrote her back this long letter, without preaching to her, telling her how much there was to live for, that she could do this or that. She wrote me back, said thank you and explained what she was feeling at the time. She let it go at that. That was nice, but it also was scary. Who am I to be giving advice to these people? I'm no social worker—I can't play God. I'm just a guy with a job.

It's pretty stressful. I feel bad that I can't answer all my own fan mail, but you can't be everyone's best friend—you just don't have the time. I understand the impulse, though, because I was the same way when I was a kid. The difference was, the people I'd always looked up to or had been interested in were either dead or had committed suicide; they were victims of mental torment. I feel mentally tormented a lot, but I think everyone does—they just won't admit it. I think everyone is pretty wacked-out in their own way.

When I start to freak out and have anxiety attacks, I smoke a lot of cigarettes and listen to very loud music. I like Bach, the Georgia Satellites, Led Zeppelin and Tom Waits—I *love* Tom Waits. When I was a kid, I did a lot of drugs when I freaked out, but I'm totally straight now.

I mean, I was in a rock & roll band in Florida, cocaine capital of the world, and drugs are really prominent in the club scene, but especially there. One day I looked around me and realized drugs weren't getting me anywhere. They were hurting me physically and mentally. They were dragging me down; they were killing me. I quit, and now I just smoke like a fiend.

Now my life revolves around work. I want to try to do as much as I can; I want to do things differently; I want to experiment; I want so express things as they never been expressed before. I'd love to play, for instance, the cockroach in Kafka's *The Metamorphosis*. It's never been done, and anyway, maybe I *am* a cockroach.

I have not even been born yet as an actor; I'm still an embryo, I'm still forming. I hope I always continue to grow. I don't want to ever get to the point where I feel completely satisfied, because, if I do, I think it's all over.

Lisa Marie

When my mom and dad met each other, she was 16 and he was 25. She was a virgin and had never had a boyfriend before; he was gorgeous and drove all the girls crazy. My mom got pregnant, and even though she and my father really didn't get along or love each other, she didn't believe in abortion, and she decided to have me.

They got married at a courthouse somewhere in the middle of the night. They had to do it for their parents. I'm really against that; no one should get married for anyone but themselves. Having a baby and not being married is *OK*, because most people don't work out, anyway; my dad and mom did not work out.

Until I was in first grade, my parents fought for my custody. My mother thought she could be a better parent; my father thought *he* could be a better parent. Who's to decide that? At one point it got really out of hand. My dad had me stay with a different person every month for a year to be hidden from my mom. I didn't realize what was happening, though; I had tons of love from everyone.

My dad finally got awarded custody, and we lived in a little house in New Brunswick, New Jersey. He is a very creative person, and he gave me the freedom to be creative and to try new things. After trying gymnastics, piano lessons and a lot of other activities, I decided on dance class. From first to eighth grade I took ballet class, but in sixth grade I got really serious. I went to dance school five days a week after regular school and on Saturday, too. Dancing was everything to me at that time.

I only hung out with my dance friends. I went to a private Catholic school called St. Francis Cabrini. I hated being in Catholic school; I always wanted to be in public school. My school wasn't social—it was so innocent. The kids in public school used to hang out, drink and party, but the kids in my school were sissies. Looking back, I'm glad things worked out the way they did because it gave me more time to work on dancing.

My best friend's name was Ariana. When we were in seventh grade, we started going into New York City to take [dance] class. I fell in love with Manhattan, and I knew I had to live and learn there. It was the first time in my life I felt I fit in somewhere. I wanted to dance and act, and I knew that all of the best teachers and classes were in the city; I wasn't going to settle for anything less.

After a lot of discussion with my father, I moved into my cousin's loft on West 29th Street and enrolled in a progressive high school; it was called "a school without doors." On Mondays, Wednesdays and Fridays, I took academic classes, and I also took language courses at the New School, dance classes at Martha Graham and Alvin Ailey and acting class at the Actors Institute.

Studying is so important to my growth as an actress. How can you lose anything by taking classes and learning? You can only gain. I take a little bit of knowledge from each teacher I study with and from each book I read. The cumulative effect is what makes me an individual. I'm not following another person's way. I'm not into Stella Adler, the method, Lee Strasberg or any one thing. To grow and become a diverse, dynamic person, you have to take little pieces from all things in life and not limit yourself.

The same principle applies to spiritual things in my life. I've always been, and will always be, close to God. It may sound corny, but it's a powerful thing if you're true to it. It makes your life so complete, because, in the long run, all you have is you and God—that spirit, that love.

I don't identify with any one religion or guru or anything like that. I just take a little part of everything the spiritual teachers have to offer and use it in my life. I put all of these little pieces together and make magical things with them.

The most important thing is to be honest with yourself. Everyone has bad qualities about themselves. There's no need to dwell on them, though. Work them out and grow. Use them to your advantage and benefit, learn from them. You have to struggle before you get to the bliss. Everything falls into place when the time is right. That's how I met Bruce Weber.

My cousin liked to fool around with video cameras, and one day he made a video of me dancing to "When a Man Loves a Woman" and doing a monologue—real simple. He liked it and sent it over to Bruce. My cousin is a top model and works with Bruce a lot, and he thought Bruce would like me.

He did and wanted to meet me in person. I went up to Bruce's studio on 26th Street to meet him. It was a rainy day. I was so shy, I put all of my hair in front of my face to hide myself; I had no confidence. Deep down I knew I had a lot to offer and be great at what I wanted to do, but I was so insecure.

I shook his hand and peeked out from behind my bangs, saw his eyes, and from that moment on, I fell in love with him and he fell in love with me. We've been doing great work together. First we did a *Lei* magazine spread, then I did Calvin Klein ads. That was great because it allowed me the freedom to leave my cousin's place and to live on my own.

My first film role is in Bruce's film about jazz trumpeter Chet Baker. It's not a big movie, but I feel so good about it. I sort of play myself. Every day we would wake up and not know what we were going to do. Right before we were going to film, Bruce would say, "OK, this is the way I want you to act." It's not a dramatic film; it's a different kind of film. I love being in front of a movie camera—it's emotion, you can express yourself and flow, it's a dance.

My film career will happen in its own space and time. People are so concerned with improving their lives. What they need to realize is change should begin within yourself. If everyone took a little more time to be loving and giving, then things would start getting a lot better in the world. It's that simple.

It's such a weird time. The world has gone mad with AIDS, violence and problems. People go to the movies and learn things. I want to raise awareness, move people and make things by expressing myself as an actress. I want to bring a little more love to the world.

The New Breed Filmography

WILLEM DAFOE
The Passion
Off Limits
Platoon
To Live And Die In L.A.
Streets Of Fire

PATRICK SWAYZE
Tiger Warsaw
Steel Dawn
Dirty Dancing
Youngblood
Red Dawn
Grand View U.S.A.
Uncommon Valor
The Outsiders
Skatetown U.S.A.

SEAN YOUNG
The Boost
Wall Street
No Way Out
Baby
Dune
Young Doctors In Love
Blade Runner
Stripes
Jane Austin In Manhattan

ROBERT DOWNEY, JR.
True Believers
1969
Less Than Zero
The Pick Up Artist
Johnny Be Good
Rented Lips
Greaser's Palace
Back To School
Weird Science
Tuff Turf
This America The Movie, Not The Country
Up The Academy
First Born
Baby It's You

MARY STUART MASTERSON
Mr. North
Some Kind Of Wonderful
Gardens of Stone
My Little Girl
At Close Range
Heaven Help Us
Stepford Wives

AIDAN QUINN
Crusoe
Stakeout
All My Sons
An Early Frost
The Mission
Desperately Seeking Susan
Reckless

KEANU REEVES
Prince of Pennsylvania
Permanent Record
Bill And Teds Excellent Adventure
The Night Before
River's Edge

PATRICK DEMPSEY
Sisters
In A Shallow Grave
Can't Buy Me Love
In The Mood
Heaven Help Us
Meatballs III

MARTHA PLIMPTON
Untitled Woody Allen
Running On Empty
Stars And Bars
Mosquito Coast
Goonies
River Rat

COREY FELDMAN
Long Before Tomorrow
License To Drive
Goonies 2
Lost Boys
Stand By Me
Goonies
Gremlins
Friday 13th, The Final Chapter
Friday 13th

JOHN CUSAK
8 Men Out
Tapeheads
Hot Pursuit
One Crazy Summer
Stand By Me
Better Off Dead
Journey Of Natty Gann
The Sure Thing
Grandview USA
16 Candles
Class

JENNIFER RUBIN
Bad Dreams
Permanent Record
Blueberry Hill
Nightmare On Elm Street III

COREY HAIM
Long Before Tomorrow
License To Drive
Lost Boys
Murphy's Romance
Lucas
First Born

ELIZABETH PERKINS
Big
Sweet Hearts Dance
From The Hip
About Last Night

ESAI MORALES
Bloodhounds On Broadway
La Bamba
Bad Boys

ALFRE WOODARD
Scrooge
Mandella
Extremeties
Cross Creek
Health
Remember My Name

RICK ROSSOVICH
The Witching Hour
Fast Forward
Secret Ingredient
Roxanne
Top Gun
The Terminator
The Morning After
Streets Of Fire
Lords Of Discipline

STEPHEN BALDWIN
Casualties of War
Motherland (The Beast)
The Prodigious Hickey

MELANIE GRIFFITH
Working Girl
Stormy Monday
Milagro Beanfield War
Something Wild
Body Double

D. B. SWEENEY
8 Men Out
No Man's Land
Gardens Of Stone

DONOVAN LEITCH, JR.
The Blob
The In Crowd
And God Created Women

DON HARVEY
Casualties Of War
Eight Men Out
Motherland (The Beast)
The Untouchables
Creep Show II

KYLE MACLACHLAN
Dune
Blue Velvet
The Hidden

LAURA DERN
Haunted Summer
Blue Velvet
Teachers
Smooth Talk
Mask
Foxes

IONE SKYE
A Day In The Life Of Jimmy Reardon
Stranded
River's Edge

COURTNEY COX
Masters Of The Universe

LARRY FISHBURNE
School Daze
Red Heat
Nightmare On Elm Street III
Gardens Of Stone
The Color Purple
Quicksilver
Cotton Club
Rumble Fish
Death Wish II
Apocalypse Now
Willie And Phil
Fast Break
Cornbread Earl and Me

RODNEY HARVEY
Salsa
Throwback
5 Corners
The Initiation
Return Of Billy Jack
Delivery Boys
Mixed Blood

JOHNNY DEPP
Platoon
Nightmare On Elm Street

LISA MARIE
The Chet Baker Story

Acknowledgments

I would like to thank the following people for their assistance to me with THE NEW BREED:

Jo Manuel, my agent, for sticking by me, for her honesty and support.

Lisa Lienhardt, Assistant to Joe Manuel, for her help, constant support and cheeriness.

Henry Holt and Company, Inc.

Peter Bejger, my editor at Henry Holt, Inc., for being so wonderful to work with, and for his belief in me throughout.

Keven J. Koffler, who I had to push at times, but who ultimately always came through for me. This was a true collaboration.

Wesley Anderson, for doing such a wonderful job designing this book and for supporting me.

Jeffrey Fields, for assisting with the design and lay-outs.

Elisabeth Feiss, for her creative input in the beginning and throughout the project.

Bud Scoppa, for being an indispensable copy editor.

Franz of Jose Éber

Tripp N.Y.C., for providing clothes for Martha Plimpton's spread.

Lynn Goldsmith

Marie Tobias at LGI

Cliff, Harry and Mark, for the use of their Cadillac.

Paul Robinson, for assisting me with the cover.

Tad Rabichaux, for transcribing.

Steven Shapiro, Esq./Mantel and Shapiro

Elizabeth Jones, for doing such great prints.

Ben Ness Photo, N.Y.C.

Photo Impact, Los Angeles

I would like to thank the following people for their assistance and support:

Phylis Carlyle Management
Erik Magrath at Phylis Carlyle Management
Ed Limato at William Morris
Michael Schulman at Ed Limato's office
Georgette Lebitty at Ed Limato's office
J. J. Harris at William Morris
Black Sox Inc.
Karen Fried at Dick Delson & Associates
Bruce Bahrenburg, unit publicist for *Motherland* and *Kansas*
Jeff Ballard
Bill Unger/Bill Unger Management
Jim Dobson/Jim Dobson & Associates
Alan Summers
Patrick Reeves
Judy Hoffland at CAA
Judy Thomas
Irwin Stoff Agency
Heidi at Irwin Stoff Agency
Hogan Scheffer
David Lewis at ICM
Lee Guthrie
Paul Kaufman
Ann Geddes Agency, thanks to Ann, Susan Dewald and Ina.
Lemmond Zetter Agency/Jim Tunnel
Helen Sugland of Land Mark Artist Management
La La Zappa
Judy Haim
Meladie Corenbrat
John Grison
John Kelly
Ened Karl
Stephanie Spring at Girlie Pictures
Susan Bymel Agency
Vic Ramos
Barbara Binstein
Jeremy Court at Wood Foley Management

I would like to thank my family and friends for supporting me, challenging me and being there:

Charlotte Ballard, my mother, for being there for me in so many ways.
Varda Hardy
Patrick Bennet
Chrystie Hardy Ballard
Verne Ballard
David Barkar
Alice, Rodney, Anthony, Matthew and Diana Kuhns
Oma, from Kevin, for love and support and for always being there.
Nick Sheridan
Chelsea
Jim Dobson
Scott Failla
Verena Schick
Andrea Lambsdorff
Steve Baldwin
Jon Wolfman
Alan Boyce
Guy McCarter
Gianna Renaudo
Frank Nielson
Paul Vrebolovich
Richard Mensing
All my friends in Norway
Jesse Kornbluth
Alex Abramowitz
Ne Omi Evan
Steven Goldstein

In addition, I would like to thank:

Gerald L'Ecuyer
Les Stickles
Vicki Bonomo
Patrick Swayze
Robert Downey, Jr.
Corey Haim
Shakti Gawain, for writing *Creative Visualization* and *Living in the Light*.
Hannes Schick